Number 154
Summer 2017

New Directions for Evaluation

Paul R. Brandon
Editor-in-Chief

Building Capacities to Evaluate Health Inequities: Some Lessons Learned from Evaluation Experiments in China, India and Chile

Sanjeev Sridharan
Kun Zhao
April Nakaima
Editors

Building Capacities to Evaluate Health Inequities: Some Lessons Learned from Evaluation Experiments in China, India and Chile
Sanjeev Sridharan, Kun Zhao, and April Nakaima (eds.)
New Directions for Evaluation, no. 154
Editor-in-Chief: *Paul R. Brandon*

New Directions for Evaluation, (ISSN 1097-6736; Online ISSN: 1534-875X), is published quarterly on behalf of the American Evaluation Association by Wiley Subscription Services, Inc., a Wiley Company, 111 River St., Hoboken, NJ 07030-5774 USA.
Postmaster: Send all address changes to *New Directions for Evaluation*, John Wiley & Sons Inc., C/O The Sheridan Press, PO Box 465, Hanover, PA 17331 USA.

Information for subscribers
New Directions for Evaluation is published in 4 issues per year. Institutional subscription prices for 2017 are:
Print & Online: US$484 (US), US$538 (Canada & Mexico), US$584 (Rest of World), €381 (Europe), £304 (UK). Prices are exclusive of tax. Asia-Pacific GST, Canadian GST/HST and European VAT will be applied at the appropriate rates. For more information on current tax rates, please go to www.wileyonlinelibrary.com/tax-vat. The price includes online access to the current and all online backfiles to January 1st 2013, where available. For other pricing options, including access information and terms and conditions, please visit www.wileyonlinelibrary.com/access.

Delivery Terms and Legal Title
Where the subscription price includes print issues and delivery is to the recipient's address, delivery terms are **Delivered at Place (DAP)**; the recipient is responsible for paying any import duty or taxes. Title to all issues transfers FOB our shipping point, freight prepaid. We will endeavour to fulfil claims for missing or damaged copies within six months of publication, within our reasonable discretion and subject to availability.

Back issues: Single issues from current and recent volumes are available at the current single issue price from cs-journals@wiley.com.

Publisher: New Directions for Evaluation is published by Wiley Periodicals, Inc., 350 Main St., Malden, MA 02148-5020.

Journal Customer Services: For ordering information, claims and any enquiry concerning your journal subscription please go to www.wileycustomerhelp.com/ask or contact your nearest office.
Americas: Email: cs-journals@wiley.com; Tel: +1 781 388 8598 or +1 800 835 6770 (toll free in the USA & Canada).
Europe, Middle East and Africa: Email: cs-journals@wiley.com; Tel: +44 (0) 1865 778315.
Asia Pacific: Email: cs-journals@wiley.com; Tel: +65 6511 8000.
Japan: For Japanese speaking support, Email: cs-japan@wiley.com.
Visit our Online Customer Help available in 7 languages at www.wileycustomerhelp.com/ask

Production Editor: Meghanjali Singh (email: mesingh@wiley.com).

Wiley's Corporate Citizenship initiative seeks to address the environmental, social, economic, and ethical challenges faced in our business and which are important to our diverse stakeholder groups. Since launching the initiative, we have focused on sharing our content with those in need, enhancing community philanthropy, reducing our carbon impact, creating global guidelines and best practices for paper use, establishing a vendor code of ethics, and engaging our colleagues and other stakeholders in our efforts. Follow our progress at www.wiley.com/go/citizenship

View this journal online at wileyonlinelibrary.com/journal/ev

Wiley is a founding member of the UN-backed HINARI, AGORA, and OARE initiatives. They are now collectively known as Research4Life, making online scientific content available free or at nominal cost to researchers in developing countries. Please visit Wiley's Content Access - Corporate Citizenship site: http://www.wiley.com/WileyCDA/Section/id-390082.html

Printed in the USA by The Sheridan Group.

Address for Editorial Correspondence: Editor-in-chief, Paul R. Brandon, New Directions for Evaluation, Email: brandon@hawaii.edu

Abstracting and Indexing Services
The Journal is indexed by Academic Search Alumni Edition (EBSCO Publishing); Education Research Complete (EBSCO Publishing); Higher Education Abstracts (Claremont Graduate University); SCOPUS (Elsevier); Social Services Abstracts (ProQuest); Sociological Abstracts (ProQuest); Worldwide Political Sciences Abstracts (ProQuest).

Cover design: Wiley
Cover Images: © Lava 4 images | Shutterstock

For submission instructions, subscription and all other information visit:
wileyonlinelibrary.com/journal/ev

Editorial Policy and Procedures

New Directions for Evaluation, a quarterly sourcebook, is an official publication of the American Evaluation Association. The journal publishes works on all aspects of evaluation, with an emphasis on presenting timely and thoughtful reflections on leading-edge issues of evaluation theory, practice, methods, the profession, and the organizational, cultural, and societal context within which evaluation occurs. Each issue of the journal is devoted to a single topic, with contributions solicited, organized, reviewed, and edited by one or more guest editors.

The editor-in-chief is seeking proposals for journal issues from around the globe about topics new to the journal (although topics discussed in the past can be revisited). A diversity of perspectives and creative bridges between evaluation and other disciplines, as well as chapters reporting original empirical research on evaluation, are encouraged. A wide range of topics and substantive domains are appropriate for publication, including evaluative endeavors other than program evaluation; however, the proposed topic must be of interest to a broad evaluation audience.

Journal issues may take any of several forms. Typically they are presented as a series of related chapters, but they might also be presented as a debate; an account, with critique and commentary, of an exemplary evaluation; a feature-length article followed by brief critical commentaries; or perhaps another form proposed by guest editors.

Submitted proposals must follow the format found via the Association's website at http://www.eval.org/Publications/NDE.asp. Proposals are sent to members of the journal's Editorial Advisory Board and to relevant substantive experts for single-blind peer review. The process may result in acceptance, a recommendation to revise and resubmit, or rejection. The journal does not consider or publish unsolicited single manuscripts.

Before submitting proposals, all parties are asked to contact the editor-in-chief, who is committed to working constructively with potential guest editors to help them develop acceptable proposals. For additional information about the journal, see the "Statement of the Editor-in-Chief" in the Spring 2013 issue (No. 137).

Paul R. Brandon, Editor-in-Chief
University of Hawai'i at Mānoa
College of Education
1776 University Avenue
Castle Memorial Hall, Rm. 118
Honolulu, HI 968222463
e-mail: nde@eval.org

CONTENTS

Editors' Notes

ealth inequity can be defined as "the difference or disparity in health outcomes that is systematic, avoidable and unjust" (Braveman, 2003; Centers for Disease Control and Prevention [CDC], 2014; Whitehead, 1991). The World Health Organization report *Closing the Gap in a Generation* (2008) argues that most health inequities are avoidable and are "the result of a toxic combination of poor social policies and programmes, unfair economic arrangements, and bad politics" (p. 1). Making judgments on the role of interventions in affecting "systematic, avoidable and unjust" outcomes requires evaluative thinking (Patton, 2008), an understanding of the generative mechanisms (Pawson, 2013) that produce inequities, a theory of change that describes how the intervention can disrupt such mechanisms and a comprehensive measurement system that collects data over time on intervention processes, contexts, and outcomes.

Although our focus is on health inequities, this volume is premised on the idea that "inequity" considerations pervade all social and health programs. It is a rare program that benefits all people uniformly. There are winners and losers in most interventions. Even with interventions that have the ambition to affect all individuals in a population, planners and implementers do care strongly about ensuring that the interventions are helpful in addressing imbalances that exist in society. Two important evaluation and program planning questions relating to equity include: How can interventions be planned to address inequities? Are those who are intended to benefit from the intervention the ones who actually benefit?

One important aspect of evaluating equities is that an equity-focused evaluation is not just about average level improvements. In equity-focused evaluations, it matters *who* engages with the program; it is also important to move beyond a focus on outputs (how many individuals were served) toward a better understanding of *who* was served and where the program recipients belonged in the continuum of need. For example, if a health screening program is unable to reach individuals who are from a social group who have higher rates of the disease, it can potentially exacerbate inequities. It matters in important ways if the improvements in key outcomes are greater for individuals who have multiple disadvantages.

A second consequence of this observation is that the theory of change focused on inequities might be different from a theory of change focused on effectiveness. As noted by Solar and Irwin (2010), it is important to make a distinction between determinants of health that are focused on the *average* and determinants of health inequities that are focused on the *distribution* of health outcomes. Graham (2004) makes this important distinction: "the social factors influencing health and the social processes shaping their unequal social distribution are not the same. Policies to achieve health gain

New Directions for Evaluation, no. 154, Summer 2017 © 2017 Wiley Periodicals, Inc., and the American Evaluation Association. Published online in Wiley Online Library (wileyonlinelibrary.com) • DOI: 10.1002/ev.20242 seek aggregate improvements in the level of health determinants; policies to promote health equity address the unequal distribution of these determinants between the advantaged and disadvantaged groups" (p. 118).

Inequities and Evaluation Influence

This volume aspires to contribute to the growing literature on how evaluations can have influence (Henry & Mark, 2003a, 2003b; Herbert, 2014; Mark & Henry, 2004; Patton, 2011) on inequities. Although there is a rich evaluation literature emerging around issues of influence, there has been more limited focus around evaluation influence on equities. Although the context of the majority of the chapters is the China health system, this focus on China is complemented with discussions on evaluations of health inequity initiatives in India and Chile.

Addressing how evaluations can have influence (Mark & Henry, 2004) on inequities requires attention to be paid to the long-term dynamic processes (Sterman, 2006) by which programs, organizations, and systems can address health inequities. This means that the evaluation should not just be viewed within the narrow confines of a specific intervention—instead questions also need to be raised about building evaluation capacities of programs, organizations, and systems.

Health Systems Reform in China

Some of the chapters in this volume discuss lessons for evaluators from a project titled "Building Health Equity in China through Evaluation Capacity Building." China embarked on an ambitious program of health systems reform starting in 2009. One of the goals of the health system reform efforts in China was to reduce health inequities between urban and rural parts of China. This project is funded by the International Development Research Centre based in Canada and supported by the former Ministry of Health in China (this ministry is now called the National Health and Family Planning Commission).

In this project we were interested in exploring the types of evidence needed to act on inequities. Such evidence typically needed to go well beyond whether an intervention worked differentially for some subgroup of individuals. It implied understanding the mechanisms underlying the intervention (why did the intervention work?) and also the context and support systems necessary for the program to work (Pawson, 2013).

Toward an Ecology of Evidence for Health Inequities: Building Capacities to Address Inequities

The genesis of this volume was at the early stages of implementing the China project in our formative discussions with policymakers. Two questions were raised by policymakers that helped frame this project (and consequently this volume). What types of evidence can an evaluation generate that can help with concrete actions toward inequities? What kinds of evaluation capacities are needed to evaluate inequities? Although we were sensitive to the fact that evaluation typically provides an opportunity to provide a wide range of learning (Henry, 2000; Patton, 2011), given the lack of a systematic focus on inequities in the evaluation literature, a precise answer to these questions was difficult. These questions helped us reflect on a theory of influence by which evaluations could affect actions on health inequities. The question on the types of useful evidence provoked us to think about the connections between the varieties of evidence that could be generated from an evaluation. We used the term the "ecology of evidence" to stress the connections between the different elements of evidence that could be generated in conducting the evaluations.

The China capacity-building project also helped us think of evaluation itself as a disruptive innovation. Although there are many examples of evaluations of programmatic interventions that could disrupt existing patterns of inequities, our interest was in exploring the pathways by which evaluation itself could disrupt patterns of inequities. As noted earlier, although the literature on the influence of evaluations on "social betterment" has been of increased interest to evaluators (Henry & Mark, 2003a, 2003b; Mark & Henry, 2004), the role of evaluations in addressing equity has not been the basis of a systematic inquiry. Most evaluations of health inequity initiatives have focused on how interventions have contributed to affecting health inequities. There has been a limited focus on the pathways by which evaluation itself can contribute to reducing inequities.

This project took a theory-driven evaluation approach to evaluating health systems reform in China. It is informed by a realist evaluation perspective (Pawson, 2006; Pawson & Tilley, 1997) that proposes exploration of the configurations of context and mechanisms that might be necessary for equity outcomes to be affected. From a realist evaluation lens, central questions for our capacity-building project included: What system-level *contexts* are necessary for health inequities to be reduced? How can evaluations shed light on the multilevel *mechanisms* that might be at play in reducing health inequities? What kinds of capacities are needed for systems and individuals to address inequities?

Building on the evaluation influence literature (Henry & Mark, 2004; Mark & Henry, 2003) we developed a framework of influence to link the ecology of evidence that evaluations can generate to actions to support equity (see Figure 1).

Our primary interest in the project was to explore ways to build evaluation capacity to reduce health inequities. The evaluation capacities that we sought to build as part of this project include the following: (a) how the evaluation needs to be informed by a social determinants of health perspective; (b) developing theories of change in inequity settings; and (c) the

Figure 1. A Theory of Influence Linking Evidence and Capacity Building to Actions to Address Health Inequities

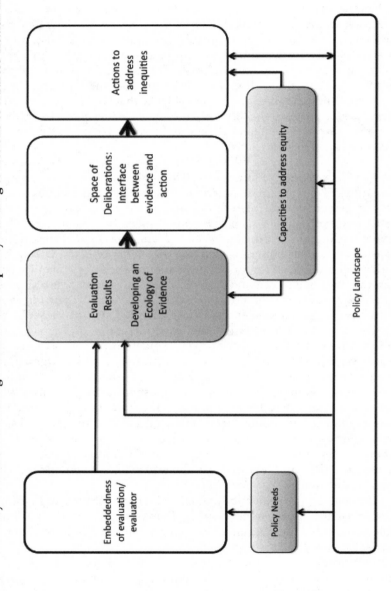

methodologies that are needed to understand impacts of system-level reforms on health inequities. One key mechanism that informed the design of the China project was learning by doing. A key challenge that the project addressed was to link the *doing* of specific evaluations to building capacities to address inequities. Many of the papers in this volume discuss the evaluation capacities needed to address inequities.

Other critical aspects of our conceptualization included understanding of the policy landscape, the drivers of the evaluation, the relationship between the evaluator and the program, and a "space" of deliberation in which issues of multiple disadvantages were considered. As these constructs are not the primary focus of this volume, we do not discuss them further here.

Description of Volume

The first five chapters discuss lessons learned from the capacity building project in China.

The introductory chapter by Kun Zhao et al. describes the theory of change that informed the evaluation capacity-building project in China. It also describes some of the challenges in thinking evaluatively about addressing inequities in China. In the spirit of evaluative thinking, this chapter raises a set of learning questions that can help measure the progress of a capacity-building project in raising the salience of equities among policymakers, practitioners, and researchers in China.

The next chapter also by Kun Zhao et al. discusses results of detailed dialogues with national and local policymakers in China on the types of issues related to equities they would hope for evaluations to address. Given our focus on evaluation influence, a good starting point is understanding the needs of policymakers. One important insight that emerges from this chapter is that policymakers in settings like China are unclear about the types of questions that evaluations can answer. A good start in building evaluation capacities to address inequities is in developing greater awareness of the types of specific information that evaluations can provide that will be useful in policy settings.

The chapter by Yue Xiao et al. describes efforts in China to build an indicator system to measure the impacts of the 12th 5-year plan. This chapter serves to highlight the ambitions of Chinese policymakers to build indicators systems to monitor and evaluate the recent health system reform efforts. It also highlights the need to develop and implement strategically designed evaluations to understand the mechanisms and impacts of specific health system reform efforts.

The chapter by Mo Yu et al. highlights lessons learned from two evaluations that were conducted in phase I of the evaluation capacity-building project in China. The intervention discussed is the New Cooperative Medical Scheme (NCMS), one of the most evaluated health initiatives in China. The two evaluations were done by local practitioners in two different provinces. The policies that were implemented within NCMS were quite different in the two provincial contexts. This chapter serves to highlight the role of evaluation in learning from implementations across different contexts.

The chapter by Sridharan et al. discusses experiences with developing structured evaluation guidelines to evaluate health inequities. These guidelines were intended to be a fixed set of questions that could be used across different interventions and across different contexts. A key lesson from this chapter is the need to move away from using such a fixed, structured approach to addressing inequities. The authors argue for a developmental approach that pays attention to the purpose of the evaluation and the context of the intervention.

In Chapters 6 through 8 our focus is on learning from evaluations in other country settings.

Katherine Hay discusses what it means for an evaluation to be disruptive. This chapter discusses an evaluation on maternal health from the Indian state of Bihar. Given the complexity of the systems in which inequities are embedded, it is important for the evaluator to recognize that our initial theories of change are often incomplete. Most programs are planned and implemented with such incomplete knowledge. Hay argues for going beyond the specific intervention as the unit of analysis toward a broader understanding of the generative mechanisms that produced the inequities. The evaluation itself can serve to make our theories of inequities more complete.

Abhijit Das focuses on evaluation of an important conditional cash transfer program in India. His message is to pay attention to the mechanisms by which an intervention such as conditional cash transfers can have unintended consequences on health equities. Das discusses the importance of an evaluator in understanding the mechanisms of change and the need to go beyond monitoring. One of the important features of this chapter is its explicit focus on the role that evaluators can play in addressing inequities.

We next turn our focus to South America and focus on learning lessons from an important capacity-building experiment in Chile. This chapter describes the lessons of a system-level theory-driven evaluation as part of a policy redesign process in Chile between 2009 and 2010. This is an important chapter because it provides one clue to how one can go beyond a specific program or policy in addressing inequities; Solar and Frenz argue that the solution might be to bring theory-driven evaluation thinking right at the policy redesign stage. The theory-driven process followed in Chile was informed by a social determinants of health perspective; the Chilean policy experiment brought groups of policy and practice stakeholders together to develop a system-level, intersectoral response to health inequities. The multistep process in Chile included steps that provided an understanding of the distribution of the social determinants of health and developed a theory of inequities that described how the system redesign could disrupt the connections between social determinants of health and health outcomes. One important contribution of this chapter is its distinction between a theory of change and a theory of inequities.

Fred Carden focuses on the challenges of building evaluation capacities to address inequities. His starting point is a recognition that evaluation capacity building is entering new territory when it addresses questions of equity. Carden recognizes that addressing inequities is an inherently political process that often challenges the status quo. Carden discusses how evaluation capacity building is critical in building knowledge of the "solution space" of inequities. An important point made by Carden is the need to move beyond the technical aspects of evaluation to the social and political dimensions of evaluation capacity building.

Finally Mel Mark explores the implications of the lessons from China, India, and Chile for how evaluations can have influence on inequities. He argues for a more contextual view of influence and explores incorporating inequities into the framework for evaluation influence (Mark & Henry, 2004). His paper serves to link our focus on the ecology of evidence and capacities to address inequities to the pathways of evaluation influence.

References

Braveman, P.A. (2003). Monitoring equity in health and healthcare: A conceptual framework. *Journal of Health, Population, and Nutrition, 21*(3), 181–192.

Centers for Disease Control and Prevention. (2014). *Social determinants of health*. Retrieved from https://www.cdc.gov/nchhstp/socialdeterminants/definitions.html

Graham, H., & East, T. (2004). Social Determinants and Their Unequal Distribution: Clarifying Policy Understandings. *The Milbank Quarterly, 82*(1), 101–124.

Henry, G. T. (2000). Why not use? In V.J. Caracelli & H. Preskill (Eds.), *New Directions for Evaluation: No. 88. The expanding scope of evaluation use* (pp. 85–98). San Francisco, CA: Jossey-Bass.

Henry, G. T., & Mark, M. M. (2003a). Beyond use: understanding evaluation's influence on attitudes and actions. *American Journal of Evaluation, 24*(3), 293–314.

Henry, G. T. & Mark, M. M. (2003b). Toward an agenda for research on evaluation. In C. A. Christie (Ed.), *New Directions for Evaluation: No. 97, The practice-theory relationship* (pp. 69–80). San Francisco, CA: Jossey-Bass.

Herbert, J. L. (2014). Researching evaluation influence: A review of the literature. *Evaluation Review, 38*(5), 388–419.

Mark, M. M., & Henry, G. T. (2004). The mechanisms and outcomes of evaluation influence. *Evaluation, 10*(1), 35–57.

Patton, M. Q. (2008). *Utilization-focused evaluation*. Thousand Oaks, CA: Sage.

Patton, M. (2011). *Developmental evaluation: Applying complexity concepts to enhance innovation and use*. New York, NY: Guilford Press.

Pawson, R. (2006). *Evidence-based policy: A realist perspective*. London: Sage.

Pawson, R. (2013). *The science of evaluation*. Thousand Oaks, CA: Sage.

Pawson R., & Tilley N. (1997). *Realist evaluation*. Thousand Oaks, CA: Sage.

Solar, O., & Irwin, A. (2010). *A conceptual framework for action on the social determinants of health* (Social Determinants of Health Discussion Paper 2 (Policy and Practice). Geneva: World Health Organization.

Sterman, J. D. (2006). Learning from evidence in a complex world. *American Journal of Public Health, 96,* 505–514.

Whitehead, M. (1991). The concepts and principles of equity and health. *Health Promotion International, 6*(3), 217–228.

World Health Organization. (2008). *Closing the gap in a generation: Health equity through action on the social determinants of health.* Commission on Social Determinants of Health–Final Report. Geneva: World Health Organization. Retrieved from http://whqlibdoc.who.int/publications/2008/9789241563703_eng.pdf?ua=1

Sanjeev Sridharan
Kun Zhao
April Nakaima

SANJEEV SRIDHARAN *is the director of The Evaluation Centre for Complex Health Interventions at St. Michael's Hospital and an associate professor with the Institute of Health Policy, Management and Evaluation at the University of Toronto in Canada.*

KUN ZHAO *is a professor at the China National Health Development Research Center in Beijing, China.*

APRIL NAKAIMA *is a senior evaluator at The Evaluation Centre for Complex Health Interventions at St. Michael's Hospital in Canada.*

Zhao, K., Sridharan, S., Ingabire, M.-G., Yu, M., Nakaima, A., Li, X., Xiao, Y., & Chen, E. (2017). An experiment on building evaluation capacity to address health inequities in China. In S. Sridharan, K. Zhao, & A. Nakaima (Eds.), *Building Capacities to Evaluate Health Inequities: Some Lessons Learned from Evaluation Experiments in China, India and Chile. New Directions for Evaluation, 154*, 17–28.

1

An Experiment on Building Evaluation Capacity to Address Health Inequities in China

Kun Zhao, Sanjeev Sridharan, Marie-Gloriose Ingabire, Mo Yu, April Nakaima, Xue Li, Yue Xiao, Emily Chen

Abstract

This paper describes an evaluation experiment conducted in China between 2013 and 2016 to use evaluative thinking and evaluation approaches to help build the salience of health equity as a performance measure for health systems. This project was informed by a realist evaluation approach that sought to understand the context, mechanisms, and outcomes underlying health inequities. This chapter describes a theory of change that includes descriptions of the key actors involved in the project, the mechanisms of impact, and short- and long-term outcomes. Key questions that could help assess the impact of this project are also discussed. This paper contributes to the literature on building evaluation capacity for health inequities. © 2017 Wiley Periodicals, Inc., and the American Evaluation Association.

T his chapter describes an evaluation capacity-building experiment to explore whether evaluation, both in its form of evaluative thinking (Patton, 2014) and the application of evaluation design, approaches, and methods, can be used as an intervention (Mark & Henry, 2004) to help raise the salience of health inequities and also lead to action toward reducing inequities. A key guiding question that informs this paper is: Can a program of evaluation help raise the salience of equities as an important criterion for judging health systems performance in a policy setting in China?

This chapter reports on the project design, including the underlying theory of change, of a project titled, "Building Health Equity in China through Evaluation Capacity Building." This project is an international collaboration between the China National Health Research Development Center (CNHRDC) and The Evaluation Centre for Complex Health Interventions (TECCHI; based in Toronto, Canada), and is funded by the International Development Research Centre (IDRC), a Canadian crown corporation. CNHDRC was the lead organization in this collaboration. CNHDRC, formerly known as the China Health Economics Institute, was established under the leadership of the Chinese Ministry of Health in 1991. The project took place between April 2013 and September 2016.

This project had strong support from the Ministry of Health in China. The long-term aspiration of some key Chinese national and provincial policymakers from this project included helping the development of a national evaluation system that consists of a variety of datasets, enhancing capacity of participating Chinese policy researchers to develop theories of change for health systems reform, developing knowledge indicators to measure progress for the health system reform, and enhancing analytical capacity of Chinese policy researchers and practitioners involved in this project.

This project builds upon an earlier phase (phase one) conducted between 2009 and 2011. The main focus of phase one was to introduce evaluation theory and design and thereby build evaluation capacity of participating Chinese policymakers and practitioners and academic researchers in evaluation theory and methodology. Phase two was intended to build on the gains from phase one and focus on evaluations of health equities of systems, policy, and program interventions.

In this chapter, we adopt the definition of health equity from the World Health Organization (2005): "The absence of unfair and avoidable or remediable differences in health among population groups defined socially, economically, demographically or geographically" (Solar and Irwin, 2010, p. 12).This definition also suggests some of the challenges in operationalizing inequities. As an example, how does one decide what is unfair, avoidable, and remediable? It is rarely a straightforward matter. Solar and Irwin (2010, p. 12) argue that "identifying a health difference as inequitable is not an objective description, but necessarily applies an appeal to ethical norms."

There have been sweeping health system reform changes in China both in 2009 and in 2012 (Hipgrave, 2011). The 2009 and the 2012 health system reform efforts aspired to reduce inequities in health between the urban and rural areas. These changes have occurred at a period of unprecedented changes in health outcomes of the Chinese health population. As an example, life expectancy at birth increased from approximately ages 35–40 in 1949 to 65.5 in 1980; in 2010 it was 76.8 for women and 72.5 for men

(Eggleston, 2012). This increase in life expectancy represents the "most rapid sustained increase in documented global history" (Eggleston, 2012, p. 2). Further, rural per capita spending increased 17-fold over the last 2 decades while the urban per capita spending increased 33-fold (China National Health Development Research Center, 2011).

Given that this project was supported by the Ministry of Health, an important issue that emerged was the role of government action for reducing inequities. Blas et al. (2008) have argued that "government action for addressing the social determinants of health inequities can take three forms: (1) as provider or guarantor of human rights and essential services; (2) as facilitator of policy frameworks that provide the basis for equitable health improvement; and (3) as gatherer and monitor of data about their populations in ways that generate health information about mortality and morbidity and data about health equity" (p. 1684). This project, although informed by Blas et al.'s insight, explored other mechanisms by which evaluation capacity building could help raise the salience of health equity among policymakers in China at the national, provincial, and local levels.

One notable feature of this project was the presence of local partners from provinces, counties, and towns. The project engaged with the local, provincial, and national policymakers around issues of marginalization and encouraged a movement away from a single factor approach to inequities toward a deeper understanding of the intersections that might lead to marginalization. Engagement with local partners was important because a point noted by many researchers was that solutions of inequities could rarely be achieved purely in a top-down fashion (Collins & Hayes, 2010).

Setting Substantive Priorities for the Project

The policy research priorities were set in meetings with national policymakers and also between the funder and the partner organizations. This meeting occurred toward the end of phase one and before the start of phase two. The dialogues focused on the role that evaluations could play to help policymakers in their task. Based on dialogues with key policymakers, six issues emerged around evaluation needs related to inequities from policymakers. These needs included greater clarity on the types of questions evaluations could answer, how evaluations of specific initiatives could be integrated with surveillance of health indicators, the role of evaluations in understanding trade-offs between equity and efficiency, build knowledge about heterogeneities of local implementations of specific initiatives, develop models of continuous improvement focused on equities, and develop knowledge of how evaluations can help move innovative results from pilots to scale. Table 1.1 describes each of these points in greater detail.

NEW DIRECTIONS FOR EVALUATION • DOI: 10.1002/ev

Table 1.1. Feedback on Policymakers' Priorities Related to Health Inequities

s

1. *Understanding the role of evaluations in planning and implementing health equity initiatives.* A number of policymakers expressed a lack of knowledge of the types of questions related to inequities that evaluations could answer. There was a desire to learn about exemplary evaluations conducted globally on health equities and the types of questions that such initiatives addressed and to clarify whether these evaluations could also be relevant to the policy and practice settings of China.

2. *Integrate evaluations of specific initiatives with routine data systems used to monitor key health indicators in China.* In China as in other countries, performance of health policy interventions is assessed through large monitoring data collection systems such as the nationwide household survey. There was an interest among policymakers to explore how such national-level surveys could be leveraged to answer evaluation questions related to health inequities.

3. *Better understand trade-offs in policy goals: balancing equity considerations with efficiency considerations.* Some of the policymakers were interested in examples of health systems that have done a good job of balancing equity with other dimensions of system performance including efficiency and effectiveness. There was a desire to learn from other health systems that had done a balanced job of simultaneously focusing on these multiple goals and how evaluations can help find such a balance. They were keen to ensure that evaluations of health system reform initiatives in China do not explore equity in isolation with other goals such as effectiveness, efficiency, and sustainability.

4. *Build knowledge about implementation.* One key area that policymakers were especially keen to know more about was the implementation of policies. Policymakers recognized that evaluations provided an opportunity to learn whether the implemented policies had fidelity to what was originally intended. Evaluations also provided an opportunity to learn more about the context of the intervention. There was also a desire among the national policymakers to learn from provincial and local practitioners about the level of detail required in national policy framework documents to help with the implementation of health equity-focused initiatives.

5. *Models of continuous improvements for health equities for existing policies.* Policymakers recognized that affecting health equities was going to be a long-term process. There was interest from policymakers to learn about evaluation methods of continuous improvement (Morell, 2000) that could help affect health equities for existing programs and policies in an ongoing way. Policymakers expressed a need to move beyond focusing on evaluation of specific episodic interventions (e.g., new pilot programs) toward methods that paid attention to continuous improvement of implementations of existing policies and programs.

6. *Moving to scale: from evaluating demonstration projects to scaling up.* There are a number of pilot programs/demonstration projects that were being implemented in China to address health inequities. Policymakers hoped to learn from these demonstration projects and were interested in how evaluations could be better structured to inform future scaling-up efforts.

The Theory of Change of the Initiative

The theory of change for this project is described in Figure 1.1.

The outcomes of this project included building capacities of organizations and participants involved in this project to conduct equity evaluations, raising the salience of equity among policymakers involved in this initiative as a performance metric of the health system, developing understanding of the drivers of inequities in health outcomes among participants, and also developing a recognition that policymaking and programming focused on equities need to explicitly plan to address inequities.

The different stakeholders who were targeted by the project included:

- Policymakers and practitioners: National, provincial, and local policymakers and practitioners were involved in this initiative. One key goal of this project was to raise the salience of health equity as a performance metric to measure the progress of the health system reforms among these stakeholders. A series of policy dialogues and interviews were conducted with local, provincial, and national policymakers and practitioners to understand their policy needs, what evaluation questions and priorities were important to them, and how equity evaluation could be best conducted to suit their needs (see Zhou et al., Chapter 2 in this volume). It was important that this project was designed not as a stand-alone project but was integrated within routine priorities in organizations. Suarez-Balcazar and Taylor-Ritzler (2014) argue that it is important that evaluation capacity building is not conceived to be a separate field but works in close congruent and reciprocal relationships with practice.
- A key goal of the project was to enhance the evaluation capacity of researchers at CNHDRC. Members of CNHDRC worked directly with the local teams in three provinces to guide the teams and provide liaison with the lead team TECCHI in Canada. Several members of CNHDRC came to Canada for several weeks and worked alongside the TECCHI team, and several members of the TECCHI team went to China on numerous occasions. CNHDRC was key to connecting all the players at all organizations and at all levels of government.
- Three teams of policymakers and researchers from the City of Wuhan, City of Qingdao in Shandong province, and Anhui province worked closely with CNHRDC and TECCHI to conduct equity evaluations of recent health system reform policies in each of the three areas. Each local evaluation team consisted of researchers (there was a local university partner for each of the teams), policymakers, and practitioners. The objectives of these evaluation projects included building local evaluation skills and knowledge, increasing awareness of equity issues for policymakers, and strengthening a culture of evidence-based decision making in the participating organizations.
- There were a number of other organizations from the national, provincial, and local levels also involved in this initiative.

NEW DIRECTIONS FOR EVALUATION • DOI: 10.1002/ev

Figure 1.1. Theory of Change of the Initiative

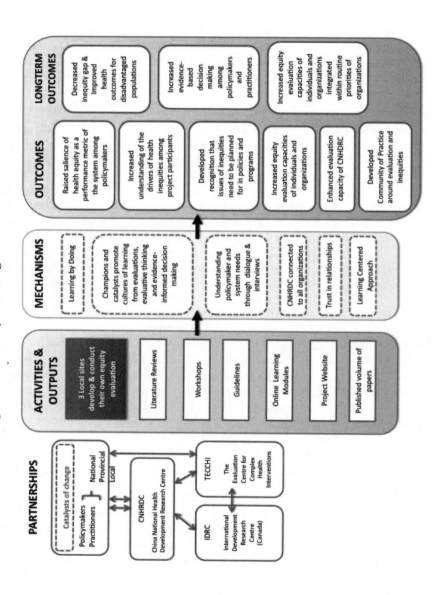

A fundamental guiding principle of the capacity-building project was *learning by doing*. This project recognized that developing a learning organization would require a long-term, holistic, participatory, learning-centered approach that aimed to develop the capacity of the whole organization; however, pragmatically we sought out a few key champions from each of the policy organizations to help promote a culture of learning from evaluations. The aspiration for each of the three teams conducting the evaluations was for the individuals involved in this initiative to be catalysts of change in their organizations. Lennie, Tacchi, Wilmore, and Koirala (2015) advocated evaluation capacity-building approaches that build the capacity of the whole organization rather than the capacity of single individuals. Suarez-Balcazar and Taylor-Ritzler (2011) argue for a catalyst for change approach in which a single staff member helps diffuse evaluation knowledge and skills within a community-based organization. Finding policymakers, managers, program staff, and researchers who were interested in the project was not hard, but gaining their commitment of time beyond a couple of meetings to learn and then conduct their own evaluations was difficult due to their time constraints.

One critical insight that guided this project was that evaluations do not by themselves lead to learning. As discussed by Taut (2007), supportive organizational contexts, structures, and processes are needed for evaluations to lead to learning. A number of workshops were directed to each of the three teams to help them learn about and from evaluations. The workshops covered a wide variety of topics including social determinants of health and health equities; formulating evaluation questions; developing evaluation designs; implementing multiple evaluation approaches including realist, developmental, and impact evaluations as they relate to health inequities; technical measures of inequities; analyzing data; and interpreting evaluation findings. The workshop activities were coordinated by CNHRDC whereas the content for the workshops was jointly developed by evaluators at TECCHI and CNHDRC.

This project was further facilitated by a series of reviews of the literature on evaluations of health inequity initiatives. Three types of reviews were completed as part of this project. One review conceptualized health equity interventions as complex interventions and explored reporting standards for complex interventions. A second set of reviews looked at the multiple evaluations of China's New Cooperative Medical Scheme (NCMS) and did a scoping review of what could be learned from the multiple evaluations of NCMS. NCMS was a public health insurance scheme adopted in 2003 to provide coverage to uninsured in rural areas. Of the multiple health system reform interventions in China, NCMS has been the most evaluated and hence most likely to lead to insights in synthesis. A third set of reviews looked at methodological standards in evaluations of health equity interventions. Each of these reviews helped build the content for the multiple workshops that were conducted as part of this initiative.

New Directions for Evaluation • DOI: 10.1002/ev

One critical product that helped facilitate the implementation of the workshops and the evaluations conducted by the local teams was the development of guidelines for evaluating health equity initiatives. These guidelines were a series of questions that each of the teams had to answer in order to evaluate the equity dimensions of the policy. Details of the evaluation guidelines are described in Chapter 8 of this volume. These guidelines were developed based on dialogue with Chinese policymakers and through reviews of the evaluation and health equity literatures.

Other activities included the development of online learning modules that could be used to introduce concepts related to evaluations of health inequities and social determinants of health to both academic and policy audiences in China and other setting. These learning modules will be piloted using an online teaching platform such as People's Uni.

A critical outcome for the project was to build a community of practice around issues of evaluation and inequities. Over the past few years, the China project has fostered a strong community whose relationships are built upon trust and a common desire to improve health care in China. Team members from CNHRDC, IDRC, and TECCHI have formed strong bonds both on professional and personal levels. Currently, the community formed by the core team has grown significantly to include a number of national policymakers who have a strong interest in health equity and close relationships with members of the core team, fellow researchers at universities in China, physicians and community leaders, and international collaborators from across the world.

Accountability Toward Learning: Questions to Assess the Performance of the Project

The three key organizations (CNHDRC, IDRC, and TECCHI) all recognized that there has been very limited research on building evaluation capacities on health inequities and there was a desire to learn from this ambitious experiment. As this initiative unfolded, a number of key guiding questions were framed to learn from this initiative. The guiding questions include:

> Did the policymakers and practitioners participating in this project recognize that the performance of a health system should at least partially be informed by the health of the most disadvantaged?

A key interest in this project was to move the focus away from an "average" level of performance of health system toward how the system was addressing the needs of the most disadvantaged individuals. Addressing this question involved numerous dialogues in the workshops around the multiple dimensions of disadvantage and how best to measure health outcomes related to multiple disadvantages.

Did the project encourage thinking of equities that went beyond a single factor explanation for equities (such as location: urban versus rural)?

One of the patterns we had noted both in the published literature on China health systems reform and among policy stakeholders in phase one of the project was the tendency to view health inequities as driven by a single factor (as example, in the literature on health inequities in China there was an implicit view that the inequities were generated by individual factors such as living in a rural area). The design of phase two was informed by a realist approach (Pawson, 2013; Pawson & Tilley, 1997) that focused on the configurations of contexts, mechanisms, and outcomes that might underlie the generation of health inequities. A critical insight from realist evaluation was that evaluations of health equity initiatives needed to focus on the generative mechanisms underlying the production of inequities. To that end, we promoted thinking about multiple levels of disadvantage and encouraged thinking of the "intersections" between different levels of disadvantage. We wanted the stakeholders to understand that the interactions between different social determinants of health (Solar & Irwin, 2010) might be responsible for the generation of inequities.

Did the project create an understanding that equity can be enhanced without a reduction in efficiency and effectiveness?

In our reading of the health systems reform literature, there was sometimes a tendency to frame equity goals at the expense of efficiency or effectiveness (Jehu-Appiah et al., 2008). We encouraged a view of health systems reform as an "optimization" problem that required both enhanced efficiencies and effectiveness and simultaneously reduced inequities. At a minimum, we wanted stakeholders to recognize that an important measure of health system performance is reduction in health inequities.

Did the project lead to recognition that addressing health inequities might require more than a single policy or program?

Many evaluations tend to be of singular programs or policies. There is an implicit tendency in some of the health equity literature to focus exclusively on single programs or policies as solutions to inequities. Given that the generative mechanisms underlying health inequities are rarely the result of a single factor or a single policy, it is unlikely that a single program or a single intervention can reverse patterns of inequities. We encouraged stakeholders to understand that addressing inequities would require implementation of multiple policies and programs over the longer term.

Did the project help stakeholders understand that projects need to be planned with intent to affect equities?

NEW DIRECTIONS FOR EVALUATION • DOI: 10.1002/ev

We were keen to treat evaluations of equity initiatives not purely as a technical problem involving post hoc (after a policy has been implemented) application of methods. Instead we promoted thinking of the inequity problem as a challenge of policy design. Policy design needed to incorporate issues of unmet need among marginalized people and the policy implementation needed to be specific in how it planned to address issues of inequities. As health systems reform was a complex, dynamic, long-term project that was implemented in an ongoing manner, it was important for the stakeholders to understand that evaluation and implementation can occur simultaneously. To this end, we also stressed developmental evaluation (Patton, 2010) as one approach to build linkages between ongoing program implementation and evaluation.

Did the project generate awareness that different types of learnings are possible from evaluations?

Although evaluations of singular interventions needed to be as useful and rigorous as possible, we encouraged thinking about what can be learned beyond a focus on the results of a single evaluation. We encouraged a focus on learning frameworks as one approach to highlight that evaluations typically can lead to a range of learnings related to inequities (Sridharan & Nakaima, 2011).

Did the project help stakeholders understand the importance of theory in assessing progress in addressing equities?

In designing this project, the team from IDRC, CNHRDC, and TECCHI felt that it was important for projects to understand that programs need a theoretical roadmap before decisions about success can be made. As part of the realist framework implemented in the capacity-building project, we stressed theoretical concepts of the pathways by which health systems reform in China could address health equities. These theoretical concepts were complemented with a focus on evaluation design and measurement to assess progress in achieving equities.

Conclusions

The funder, IDRC, and the key partners CNHDRC and TECCHI were very mindful of the fact that solutions to inequities were not going to be generated overnight or just be focused over a short term, over the course of this project. A critical interest from each of the three partners was to generate knowledge of the specific capacities that needed to be built to raise the salience of inequities as a performance metric of health care. This initiative is viewed as a learning experiment: the project is still unfolding and will likely be completed by the end of 2016. Lessons from this initiative will inform future evaluation capacity-building experiments in China. This volume of papers itself is part of building such a learning experiment.

References

Blas, E., Gilson, L., Kelly, M. P., Labonté, R., Lapitan, J., Muntaner, C., ... Vaghri, Z. (2008). Addressing social determinants of health inequities: What can the state and civil society do? *Lancet, 372*(9650), 1684–1689.

China National Health Development Research Center. (2011). *Abstract of China total health expenditure.* Beijing: Ministry of Health, People's Republic of China.

Collins, P. A., & Hayes, M. V. (2010). The role of urban municipal governments in reducing health inequities: A meta-narrative mapping analysis. *International Journal for Equity in Health, 9*(13). https://doi.org/10.1186/1475-9276-9-13

Eggleston, K. (2012). *Health care for 1.3 billion: An overview of China's health system* (Stanford Asia Health Policy Program working paper series on health and demographic change in the Asia-Pacific. Working paper # 28). Stanford, CA: Walter H. Shorenstein Asia-Pacific Research Center, Stanford University.

Hipgrave, D. (2011). Perspectives on the progress of China's 2009–2012 health system reform. *Journal of Global Health, 1*(2), 142–147.

Jehu-Appiah, C., Baltussen, R., Acquah, C., Aikins, M., d'Almeida, S. A., Bosu, W. K., ... Adjei, S. (2008). Balancing equity and efficiency in health priorities in Ghana: The use of multicriteria decision analysis. *Value Health, 11*(7), 1081–1087.

Lennie, J., Tacchi, J., Wilmore, M., & Koirala, B. (2015). A holistic, learning-centred approach to building evaluation capacity in development organizations. *Evaluation, 21*(3), 325–343.

Mark, M. M., & Henry, G. T. (2004). The mechanisms and outcomes of evaluation influence. *Evaluation, 10*(1), 35–57.

Morell, J. A. (2000). Internal evaluation: A synthesis of traditional methods and industrial engineering. *American Journal of Evaluation, 21*(1), 41–52.

Patton, M. Q. (2010). *Developmental evaluation: Applying complexity concepts to enhance innovation and use.* New York, NY: Guilford Press.

Patton, M. Q. (2014). *Evaluation flash cards: Embedding evaluative thinking in organizational culture.* St. Paul, MN: Otto Bremer Foundation.

Pawson, R. D. (2013). *The science of evaluation: A realist manifesto.* London, UK: Sage Publications.

Pawson, R. D., & Tilley, N. (1997). *Realistic evaluation.* London, UK: Sage Publications.

Solar, O., & Irwin, A. (2010). *A conceptual framework for action on the social determinants of health* (Social Determinants of Health Discussion Paper 2, Policy and Practice). Geneva: World Health Organization.

Sridharan, S., & Nakaima, A. (2011). Ten steps to making evaluation matter. *Evaluation and Program Planning, 34*(2), 135–146.

Suarez-Balcazar, Y., & Taylor-Ritzler, T. (2014). Moving from science to practice in evaluation capacity building. *American Journal of Evaluation, 35*(1), 95–99.

Taut, S. (2007). Studying Self-Evaluation Capacity. *American Journal of Evaluation, 28*(1), 45–59.

World Health Organization. (2005). "Equity Team" working definition. Health and Human Rights and Equity Working Group draft glossary. Unpublished manuscript.

KUN ZHAO *is a professor at the China National Health Development Research Center in Beijing, China.*

SANJEEV SRIDHARAN *is the director of The Evaluation Centre for Complex Health Interventions at St. Michael's Hospital and an associate professor with the Institute of Health Policy, Management and Evaluation at the University of Toronto in Canada.*

MARIE-GLORIOSE INGABIRE *is the senior program specialist at the Canada's International Development Research Centre (IDRC).*

MO YU *is a research coordinator at The Evaluation Centre for Complex Health Interventions at St. Michael's Hospital in Canada.*

APRIL NAKAIMA *is a senior evaluator at The Evaluation Centre for Complex Health Interventions at St. Michael's Hospital in Canada.*

XUE LI *is a researcher at the China National Health Development Research Center in Beijing, China.*

YUE XIAO *is a senior researcher based at the China National Health Development Research Center in Beijing, China.*

EMILY CHEN *is a researcher based at The Evaluation Centre for Complex Health Interventions at St. Michael's Hospital in Canada.*

NEW DIRECTIONS FOR EVALUATION • DOI: 10.1002/ev

Zhao, K., Nakaima, A., Wudong, G., Qiu, Y., & Sridharan, S. (2017). Evaluation at the time
of health systems reform: Chinese policymakers' need for a robust system of evaluations
to assess progress in the implementation of reform efforts. In S. Sridharan, K. Zhao, &
A. Nakaima (Eds.), *Building Capacities to Evaluate Health Inequities: Some Lessons Learned
from Evaluation Experiments in China, India and Chile. New Directions for Evaluation, 154,*
29–39.

2

Evaluation at the Time of Health Systems Reform: Chinese Policymakers' Need for a Robust System of Evaluations to Assess Progress in the Implementation of Reform Efforts

Kun Zhao, April Nakaima, Wudong Guo, Yingpeng Qiu,
Sanjeev Sridharan

Abstract

In 2014 the authors of this paper, evaluators from China and Canada, jointly interviewed 12 policymakers in China at the national and provincial levels. This paper describes the needs of policymakers and how they view the evaluation capacity-building needs of the health system. The learnings from the policymaker dialogues informed the evaluation capacity-building efforts at three pilot sites in China. This paper focuses on the evaluation capacities needed by policymakers and implementers specifically to address inequities in the health sector, unlike most publications that focus on evaluation capacities of researchers. © 2017 Wiley Periodicals, Inc., and the American Evaluation Association.

Both rich and poor countries have been seeing significant inequities in health within their populations in the last few decades. This includes China; however, this was not always the case. China made great strides in health performance since the establishment of the People's Republic of China in 1949 and was recognized internationally as an outstanding health performer in the 1970s (Tang et al., 2008). However, after 1978 when China moved toward a global economy (Dong & Phillips, 2008), health inequities began to grow. With the change in economic policy, the Eastern provinces near the coast rapidly grew in wealth whereas the Western provinces remained primarily rural and at a disadvantage to prosper economically. The economic growth overall for China brought improvements as measured by broad population health indicators such as life expectancy and infant mortality (Liu, Rao, Wu, & Gakidou, 2008); however, these indicators were averages for all of China—mortality and morbidity rates were improving at a much faster rate in the urban and Eastern provinces than in the rural and Western provinces. There was also a growing class of migrant workers from rural areas traveling to urban centers for work but not covered by health insurance schemes in the last decades. Additionally, the shift to a market-oriented health system in the 1980s and fee-for-service payment methods encouraged perverse incentives; for example, more expensive drugs, tests, and treatments were overprescribed by hospitals, which increased their profits but drove up costs to patients. Concern grew in China about the equitable distribution of social benefits, such as access to good quality health care, associated with economic growth (Tang et al., 2008).

"Health and health equity are values in their own right and are also important prerequisites for achieving many other societal goals" (World Health Organization [WHO], 2013, p. i20). In many countries the gaps in health inequities have widened in the 2 decades since the World Health Organization added "extreme poverty," a social determinant of health, to its International Classification of Diseases (WHO, 1995, p. 1) and in the decade since WHO established its Commission on Social Determinants of Health. The commission states, "Within countries there are dramatic differences in health that are closely linked with degrees of social disadvantage." This disadvantage is "shaped by political, social, and economic forces" (CSDH, 2008, introduction page).

To help address health inequities, the Chinese government sought to build its evaluation capacity. The authors of this paper interviewed Chinese national, provincial, and municipal policymakers to investigate how evaluation could be useful to them. This chapter describes the evaluation needs of key policymakers and how they view the evaluation capacity-building needs of the health system.

Unlike other published literature on evaluation capacity building (King, 2007, 2008), our focus is on evaluation capacities *to address inequities in the health sector*. And unlike the majority of the literature on evaluation capacities that focuse on capacities of researchers, this paper addresses the capacities of policymakers and the system as a whole. Additionally this paper hopes to contribute to the growing literature on how evaluations can have influence (Henry & Mark, 2003a, 2003b; Mark & Henry, 2004). By understanding policymaker needs, this paper explores influence pathways in complex political settings like the China health system and how evaluations need to be designed to have influence. Our view is that evaluations, like the interventions that they evaluate, can help in addressing issues of inequities—evaluations themselves are interventions (Henry & Mark, 2003a).

Project Background

The Chinese government has enacted a bold set of reforms in response to rising public discontent as a result of unaffordable access and widespread inequities in health care across the nation (Yip et al., 2012). Major reform areas include improving access and infrastructure of primary care and public health programs (Equalization of Public Health Services), subsidizing and improving insurance coverage (New Cooperative Medical Scheme), establishing an essential medicine program (Essential Drug List), and reducing expenditure in public hospitals.

Given the remarkable set of health system reform efforts and pilot experiments that have been and are currently being conducted in China, there has been a need not only to conduct evaluations but to build capacities for thinking evaluatively (King, 2007, 2008; Stevahn, King, Ghere, & Minnema, 2005) and to promote the use of evaluation methods and approaches both among evaluators/researchers and among policymakers and implementers.

By 2008 Chinese policymakers were interested in studying the impacts of the health system reforms, commissioning evaluations of national and local efforts. They also foresaw the need for building evaluation capacity. A collaborative project developed between the governments of China and Canada titled, "Building Health Equity in China through Evaluation Capacity Building," funded by the International Development Research Centre (IDRC) in Canada and supported by the former Chinese Ministry of Health, renamed the National Health and Family Planning Commission (NHFPC), in China. Capacity-building efforts were led collaboratively by The Evaluation Centre for Complex Health Interventions (TECCHI) in Toronto and in Beijing by the China National Health Development Research Center (CNHDRC), a national think tank providing technical consultancy to health policymakers across China. Three sites volunteered to participate in the evaluation capacity-building experiment that would allow them to conduct their own evaluation of their implementation of reforms as pilots to inform implementation in the rest of the country. Each of the three sites elected to focus on evaluating the implementation of either the Essential Drug List or the Equalization of Public Health Services.

Methodology

In August 2014, the authors interviewed 12 policymakers:

NEW DIRECTIONS FOR EVALUATION • DOI: 10.1002/ev

- Four high-level directors from the central (federal) government's National Health and Family Planning Commission were interviewed individually for about 1 hour each.
- One director and one senior staff member from the NHFPC were interviewed together for about 45 minutes.
- Two municipal policymakers were interviewed together for about 1.5 hour.
- Three provincial directors and one university lead professor were interviewed together for about 2 hours.

Interviews were conducted in four cities: Wuhan in Hubei province, Qingdao in Shandong province, Hefei in Anhui province, and the national capital Beijing.

Understanding the needs of policymakers was critical for designing capacity-building efforts. Rather than general capacity building for a general audience, the lead evaluation teams sought to design capacity-building workshops and materials to meet specific needs and train specific individuals identified by the system-level planners/ senior policymakers from both central and local levels to be available to meet the practical needs of the system moving forward. Toward this purpose, we conducted the interviews exploring the following eight questions:

1. Whose capacities need to be developed at the national and local levels?
2. What types of capacities are needed?
3. What are the baseline skills in evaluation with a focus on health equity?
4. How will stakeholders use evaluation?
5. What types of data are routinely collected at the local and national levels currently?
6. How can this project build a culture in which programmatic targets are viewed through an equity lens?
7. Are policymakers using evaluation results to make decisions?
8. How can this project be useful to this policymaker?

The interviews were audio recorded. One evaluator typed the notes and organized the responses by individual responses as well as a synthesis of key points for each of the eight questions and made note of implications for the capacity-building efforts moving forward. Another Canadian evaluator and two Chinese evaluators then reviewed the notes and added their reflections and clarifications.

Key Points

The key points that emerged from the interviews are discussed in this section.

NEW DIRECTIONS FOR EVALUATION • DOI: 10.1002/ev

Conceptual Challenges Related to Equity

The multiple meanings of "equity"were not clear to local policymakers and their staff at the beginning of our meetings. Policymakers wanted a better understanding of the multiple types of inequity issues, how they differ, and the logic by which one chooses to focus on one type of inequity over another. Based on these discussions, the guidelines that were developed for evaluating health equity initiatives (see Chapter 5 in this volume by Sridharan et al.) strove to clearly provide examples of different types of inequities. A point noted by a provincial director was that there was a difference between trying to understand *access* in terms of the *price* of medications and the *expense* for the patient—for example, even though medication prices may come down with the Essential Drug List initiative that does not mean that medication will be more affordable for many patients. She also pointed out several possible unintended outcomes of the policy initiative, e.g., that high demand for the drugs on the Essential Drug List would drive up the cost of the drugs because of market supply-and-demand forces or that manufacturing quality might go down because the drug sales are guaranteed to remain high or because manufacturers have to rush production to keep up with demand.

Further discussions about the difference between "equity" and "equalization" came up with local groups because strategies such as the Essential Drug List and the Equalization of Public Health Services are examples of *equalization* where all provinces, rich and poor, urban and rural, receive the same amount of funding per capita from the central government and are to deliver the same package of services to citizens (with some adaptation allowed for local needs). However, provincial directors brought up the concern that there are political, ethical, and accountability tensions associated with focusing on equity (as in providing disproportionate services to those based on need) versus equalization (treating all individuals uniformly). From a social determinants of health perspective, there was a recognition that individuals who are at the more disadvantaged segment of the health gradient need disproportionately more resources to bring them up to par with more advantaged segments of the population. However, there was a robust discussion around concerns that a system that allows disproportionate distribution could open the doors to corruption.

A second conceptual difficulty for policymakers was that their usual focus is primarily on efficiency, given their responsibilities for budgetary accountability. Much of the focus on measuring performance in China has been on efficiency. Stakeholders were keen to learn how health systems could balance a focus on efficiency and equity. A point noted by some local directors was that they first try for effectiveness and efficiency and then move toward equity. However, a critical question raised by some stakeholders was whether systems focused on equity could also become more efficient.

NEW DIRECTIONS FOR EVALUATION • DOI: 10.1002/ev

Raising Awareness

Many stakeholders felt that health equity was a core issue but not yet a big part of decision makers' daily worlds. Many stakeholders at all levels of government reflected on examples of initiatives that were never discussed in terms of "equity" but that actually did target equitable outcomes. One central government stakeholder noted the need to educate people across all levels of government about health equity. This policymaker always endeavors to include at least one measure or one story highlighting equity in every presentation she makes to raise the salience of health equity with other policymakers. There was interest in raising awareness of equity locally, including by academic collaborators. A point that was stressed by multiple stakeholders was that awareness about health equities was needed before they could learn about the equity-focused methodology.

At a more basic level, some stakeholders mentioned that there is a lack of clarity about what evaluations are and how they can be useful. A couple of stakeholders who attended the evaluation workshops in an earlier phase of the evaluation capacity-building partnership between China and Canada said that those workshops had expanded their understanding of the scope and value of evaluations. However, it was not clear to them why health equity was important enough to commit already constrained human resources to first learn how to evaluate health equities and then to conduct the evaluations.

Primary Concerns of Local Policymakers

Along the lines of the point that policymakers primarily focus on efficiency, one local director stated that at the most basic level as a policymaker, if he invests, he wants to know what results he will get for his investment. Evaluation for him was useful in being able to better determine value for money spent. Similarly, there was an interest from another local policymaker in using evaluations to achieve results in a timely manner. Policymakers cannot always wait 2 years for a research study to be completed for evidence to base decisions on and to take action, so frequent feedback of data and indications of results were more useful to them than high quality research too late. United Kingdom (UK) policymakers echoed similar needs in a study conducted more than a decade ago:

> Participants specifically identified a need for evaluations of the effectiveness and cost-effectiveness of policy and other interventions to reduce health inequalities. Predictive research was also seen as important (for example modelling the effects of globalisation, and simple predictive models to help identify "best buys"). (Petticrew, Whitehead, Macintyre, Graham, & Egan, 2004, p. 813)

Chinese policymakers were not solely concerned with cost effectiveness. Some stakeholders wanted to obtain feedback from citizens about how they can optimize quality. Some policy stakeholders were keen to see if the new set of reforms resulted in enhanced equity of use between urban and rural areas. Much of the focus of the health system reforms have been on access and use. In the discussions with local policymakers and their staff, it was noted that they were thinking of access and use in terms of averages and were not sure, at that time, how or why data needed to be stratified to better understand inequities. Local policymakers also expressed interest in learning about equity indicators from international settings, including recommendations of the World Health Organization.

Concerns of National-Level Policymakers

Although rich data were available and database capacities were substantial at both the local and national levels, all of the national-level policymakers emphasized capacity needs around more advanced analysis, a notion of "deep analysis," how to get more from the rich data, how to select the right groups of methods and indicators to arrive at results, and specific methods to evaluate equity issues and public health services for equity. For indicators one director felt strongly that gender and child considerations should be included at every level of programming, in all districts and pilots. Her recommendation is in line with the Millennium Development Goals (United Nations [UN], 2000) although she did not make reference to the MDGs.

One policymaker stressed that researchers need to learn how to write recommendations for policymakers. This feedback was consistent with the views of UK policymakers who were interviewed by Petticrew et al. (2004) and recommended that researchers should write their reports in a clearly stated format, keeping in mind the time constraints of policymakers. They also noted that policymakers value a "good story" along with other evidence. Additionally:

> There was much doubt among the group about the value of a "hierarchy of evidence" in public health as used in evidence based health care. They noted again the problem with "high concept" notions of evidence preferred by academics, and pointed out that in policy circles a "mixed economy" of evidence actually prevailed, in which different types of experimental and non-experimental evidence are brought to bear on policy questions. It was felt that researchers therefore need to help policymakers with managing this mixed economy; for example, to help deal with many small pieces of evidence, of variable quality, (and with many gaps), but all pointing in the same direction. (Petticrew et al., 2004, p. 813)

Integrated Evaluation and Knowledge Translation: Implementation Needs

There was a very strong interest in learning about implementation. National-level policymakers were keen to see capacities built at the local level around implementation and knowledge translation, both of which reciprocally inform and can be informed by evaluation. One director suggested that it would be helpful if pilot projects could verify a perspective of evaluation and methodology that could be transplanted to nationwide evaluations—thus using the pilots to help develop a framework for spread. He also implied that monitoring and evaluation are used mostly at the national level; he listed a host of capacity needs at the local level: *knowledge and skill in strategic planning, implementation, improvement know-how, how to use evidence, how to collect data, how to develop strategies and define success for their local context while aligning with the general intent of the central government policy statement.* Another director offered a similar assessment of local capacity needs and also wanted to learn about *incentives, unintended outcomes, motivation, and mobilization on the ground.* The problem area he identified was implementation at the local level in accordance with the plans/design of the central government. He recognized that without monitoring and evaluation expertise, plans cannot be implemented "properly, economically, rationally." Evaluation also would be useful for him in his policy planning work to help detect what may be very difficult to change and what might be the most changeable target in the next 5 years.

Ground Realities that Facilitate and Hinder

Both staff and policymakers, especially at the local level, were very busy and thus had limited capacity in terms of not enough human resources or time to get involved in evaluations. Until this project had started, directors at all levels of government said that they normally invited other parties to do evaluations for them. When it was suggested by one policymaker that perhaps it would be better to simply train researchers from the university because his staff did not have time, the lead academic researcher in that province countered with the suggestion that policymakers and managers need to be trained along with researchers because otherwise the policymakers and managers will not understand the results presented by the researchers. This comment relates to the capacity needs cited by the national director who felt that local governments needed to learn *how to use evidence, how to develop strategies and define success for their local context*—essentially evaluative thinking. The comment also may hint at the disconnection between what researchers tend to focus on and their typical manner of reporting versus what policymakers need.

Some policymakers felt that there was not much support for evaluation, mostly because they believed that there was a systemwide lack of understanding of what evaluation is and the value it adds. Other likely factors for lack of support for evaluation in China include the scarcity of human resources and a focus on monitoring systems at the expense of evaluation. For monitoring, several national surveillance systems are in place—e.g., one department collects monthly data from 700,000 grassroots community health agencies. Education is still needed across sectors on the importance of equity and the usefulness of evaluations.

Emergent Ideas

There was recognition among policymakers that changes in equity are seen as progress on a "long march." The evaluation capacity building itself was seen as a long march.

Interesting concepts emerged from the interviews including "equity distance"—e.g., the equity distance between rural and urban populations, implying one measure summing the many factors that contribute to a gap in equitable outcomes between the two populations. Another insight was captured by the concept of "capacity for collaboration"—encompassing elements of interpersonal skills, communication, interprofessional and intersectoral alliances, shared vision, organizational structures, processes and values, and time allowing for collaboration. Given the understanding that health inequities are driven by broader societal factors beyond the health system, the need for *capacity for collaboration* is extremely important. Consider what the Health in All Policies (HiAP) Framework for Country Action developed by the World Health Organization recommends:

> Many of the determinants of health and health inequities in populations have social, environmental and economic origins that extend beyond the direct influence of the health sector and health policies. Thus, public policies in all sectors and at different levels of governance can have a significant impact on population health and health equity. [...] They should therefore actively seek opportunities to collaborate with and influence other sectors. Intergovernmental organizations and structures (multi-lateral, bilateral, regional, etc.) can provide significant support to multi-sectoral action on health and development outcomes. (WHO, 2013, p. i19)

Conclusion

This paper summarizes feedback from policymakers, seeking to better understand their needs for the types of capacity they would like to have built to address inequities in China. The lead evaluation teams generated a list of "action items" to move the evaluation capacity building forward based on the learning on the needs of policymakers for system impacts. Included here is a selection of those action items:

- The evaluation teams need to leverage existing networks and develop a clear influence framework by which the project can have influence at the national and local levels.
- Health equity indicators need to be included in monitoring systems.
- If equity evaluation guidelines can be developed based on the Chinese context during the progress of the project, then these guidelines may con-

tribute and have influence nationally as other provinces implement the policy reforms.

• Ideally the lessons learned from the three pilot sites should help inform a national strategy for both spreading evaluation practice and implementing the policy reforms.

• More needs to be done across multiple sectors of government, not just the health sector, in order that policymakers can become aware of the value and usefulness of evaluations and the importance of addressing health inequities.

This paper highlights the need for evaluation capacity building to be considered as an explicit and distinct process in how evaluations can have influence. The challenge is that as evaluations of specific programs occur, how can evaluation capacities of key stakeholders who are also being evaluated be built? Although the influence framework described by Henry and Mark (2003a) is in terms of influence of individual evaluations, the findings from this paper suggest that the framework could include evaluation capacity-building activities and participation in evaluation processes. In thinking about evaluation influence, one might be tempted to conceive of the pathway as tending to start from an individual-level influence toward collective outcomes, where for example an individual influenced by an evaluation report shares the findings with others and then collective action might follow. Collectively IDRC, CNHDRC and TECCHI sought through this project to influence individuals and collectives of individuals, particularly at the local level, to raise salience, elaboration, attitude change, skill acquisition, and persuasion and for change agents or champions to emerge.

The feedback received from the Chinese policymakers can help design other programs of evaluation capacity building focused on equities. We believe the relevance of some of this feedback goes well beyond China.

References

CSDH. (2008). *Closing the gap in a generation: Health equity through action on the social determinants of health*. Final Report of the Commission on Social Determinants of Health. Geneva: World Health Organization. Retrieved from http://www.who.int/social_determinants/thecommission/finalreport/en/

Dong, Z., & Phillips, M. R. (2008). Evolution of China's health-care system. *The Lancet, 372*(9651). https://doi.org/10.1016/S0140-6736(08)61351-3

Henry, G. T., & Mark, M. M. (2003a). Beyond use: Understanding evaluation's influence on attitudes and actions. *American Journal of Evaluation, 24*(3), 293–314. https://doi.org/10.1177/109821400302400302

Henry, G. T., & Mark, M. M. (2003b).Toward an agenda for research on evaluation. In C. A. Christie (Ed.), *New Directions for Evaluation: No. 97. The practice–theory relationship* (pp. 69–80). San Francisco, CA: Jossey-Bass. https://doi.org/10.1002/ev.77

King, J. A. (2007). Developing evaluation capacity through process use. In J. B. Cousins (Ed.), *New Directions for Evaluation: No. 116. Process use in theory, research, and practice* (pp. 45–59). San Francisco, CA: Jossey-Bass. https://doi.org/10.1002/ev.242

King, J. A. (2008). Bringing evaluative learning to life. *American Journal of Evaluation, 29*(2), 151–155. https://doi.org/10.1177/1098214008316423

Liu, Y., Rao, K., Wu, J., & Gakidou, E. (2008). Health system reform in China 7: China's health system performance. *The Lancet, 372*, 1914–1923. https://doi.org/10.1016/S0140-6736(08)61362-8

Mark, M. M., & Henry, G. T. (2004). The mechanisms and outcomes of evaluation influence. *Evaluation, 10*(1), 35–57. https://doi.org/10.1177/1356389004042326

Petticrew, M., Whitehead, M., Macintyre, S. J., Graham, H, & Egan, M. (2004). Evidence for public health policy on inequalities: 1: The reality according to policymakers. *Journal of Epidemiology and Community Health, 58*, 811–816. https://doi.org/10.1136/jech.2003.015289

Stevahn, L., King, J. A., Ghere, G., & Minnema, J. (2005). Establishing essential competencies for program evaluators. *American Journal of Evaluation, 26*(1), 43–59. https://doi.org/10.1177/1098214004273180

Tang, S., Meng, Q., Chen, L., Bekedam, H., Evans, T., & Whitehead, M. (2008). Health system reform in China 1: Tackling the challenges to health equity in China. *The Lancet, 372*, 1493–1501. https://doi.org/10.1016/S0140-6736(08)61364-1

United Nations Millennium Project. (2000). *Goals, target, and indicators.* Retrieved from http://www.unmillenniumproject.org/goals/gti.htm

World Health Organization. (2013). Health in All Policies (HiAP) framework for country action. Conference outcome documents. *Health Promotion International, 29*(1), i19–i28.

World Health Organization. (1995). *The World Health Report 1995: Bridging the gaps.* Report of the Director-General. Geneva: World Health Organization.

Yip, W. C., Hsiao, W. C., Chen, W., Hu, S., Ma, J., & Maynard, A. (2012). Early appraisal of China's huge and complex health-care reforms. *Lancet, 379*(9818), 833–842. https://doi.org/10.1016/S0140-6736(11)61880-1

KUN ZHAO *is a professor at the China National Health Development Research Center in Beijing, China.*

APRIL NAKAIMA *is a senior evaluator at The Evaluation Centre for Complex Health Interventions at St. Michael's Hospital in Canada.*

WUDONG GUO *is a researcher at the China National Health Development Research Center in Beijing, China.*

YINGPENG QIU *is a researcher based at the China National Health Development Research Center in Beijing, China.*

SANJEEV SRIDHARAN *is the director of The Evaluation Centre for Complex Health Interventions at St. Michael's Hospital and an associate professor with the Institute of Health Policy, Management and Evaluation at the University of Toronto in Canada.*

Xiao, Y., Zhao, K., Sridharan, S., & Cao, X. (2017). Conceptual indicators framework for strengthening the Chinese health system. In S. Sridharan, K. Zhao, & A. Nakaima (Eds.), *Building Capacities to Evaluate Health Inequities: Some Lessons Learned from Evaluation Experiments in China, India and Chile. New Directions for Evaluation, 154*, 41–53.

3

Conceptual Indicators Framework for Strengthening the Chinese Health System

Yue Xiao, Kun Zhao, Sanjeev Sridharan, Xiaohong Cao

Abstract

In 2009 the national government of China launched massive health reforms, together with other social and economic reforms. For the first time, evaluation was included in the draft national plan of health reforms and development—the so-called "12th Five-Year National Plan for Health Development (2011– 2015)." The Chinese and Canadian researchers, with the support of the International Development Research Centre, Canada, helped to facilitate a deliberative process by various actors by conceptualizing an indicators system and mapping out key questions to be addressed by evaluating implementation of the national health plan. The conceptual indicators system serves as a platform for users and implementers of evaluation program to understand needs for evaluation better and sharpen focus on more prominent dimensions such as equity and contextual analysis. © 2017 Wiley Periodicals, Inc., and the American Evaluation Association.

For decades, evaluations were judged in terms of technical quality, methodological rigor, and utility, and actual use of evaluations was mostly ignored (Patton, 2008). With increasing emphasis on accountability and evidence-based decision making, there has been a surge of need for utilization-focused evaluations. Utilization-focused evaluation is "done for and with specific intended primary users for specific, intended uses" (Patton, 2008, p. 37). In conducting such type of evaluations, evaluators are supposed to interact and work with intended users, helping them to understand needs and identify the most suitable content, model, method, theory, and use of a particular evaluation project. Mapping out intended users, different evaluation purposes, key questions, and factors affecting use shall come before finding evaluation approaches and methods. An overall framework systematically capturing complexities is key to making evaluations useful for the intended users. It is the basis for the design of an evaluation and provides directions for implementing evaluation activities. An evaluation framework can be used practically for summarizing and organizing main processes of effective evaluation (Centers for Disease Control and Prevention, 2016).

This chapter documents the process of developing an indicator framework for evaluating health systems strengthening in China, providing a case on developing a utilization-focused evaluation thinking right at the beginning. Discussions in the chapter are conceptual rather than operational, aiming to develop a platform for engaging evaluators and target users of evaluation in debates.

Rationale for a Conceptual Indicators Framework

Since the early 2000s, the Chinese government has begun to pay increasing attention to health system strengthening and has established various reform programs in accordance (Alva, Kleinau, Pomeroy, & Rowan, 2009). In April 2009, it announced the launch of a comprehensive health systems reform agenda, with the goal of achieving affordable universal healthcare by 2020 (Yip et al., 2012). Some health policymakers describe the reform as "a gigantic systems engineering work," featured with great complexity. It is meant to initiate changes in four main functional parts (financing, public health, healthcare service delivery, and essential drugs), and try to establish appropriate mechanisms to maintain functions of these subsystems, which call for nuanced design and careful implementation to balance interests of different actors and agents, and build up relevant systems and mechanisms.

A consistent and systematic framework is important for assessing the performance of health systems (Murray & Frenk, 2000; WHO, 2000). In 2011, a team of researchers from the China National Health Development Research Center (CNHDRC)—a national health policy think tank, in collaboration with the International Development Research Centre (IDRC) of Canada developed an indicator framework for assessing health systems strengthening in China (2011–2020). This project coincided with another project on indicators system for the 12th Five-Year Plan (2011–2015) for Health Development commissioned by the Department of Planning and Information, National Health and Family Planning Commission (NHFPC; formerly known as the Ministry of Health) of China. This was the first time that the national health authority in China formally commissioned an evaluation of 5-year plans for health. Policy accountability was stressed in public service management reforms, and evaluation began to be viewed as a tool for supporting evidence-based decision making. Requirements for monitoring and evaluation were described vaguely in a few lines at the end of the draft health plan, and the health planners were not so sure about what evaluation can do for the plan. In the draft document prepared by the health planners there were already some indicators identified through a deliberation process.

Against such a background, the CNHDRC and Canadian experts decided to conceptualize an indicators framework of practical use to the health decision makers, that is to help the health planners, program designers, and local decision makers to sort out draft indicators and better understand their need for evaluation.

Framing an Indicators System

After discussions with key policymakers and experts, a general utilization evaluation approach was taken to develop the indicators system, with engagement of target users of the indicators. The research team promised to develop a framework by collectively working with decision makers and program implementers at central, provincial, municipal, and county levels. Several principles were agreed to keep the evaluation indicators more of practical use. First, the framework needed to reflect values and priorities of current health reforms. Second, the framework had to capture needs of different parts and layers of the Chinese health system. Third, the framework could be useful as a common ground to facilitate communications between various stakeholders and accommodate future changes.

With its focus on understanding evaluation needs of users, a utilization evaluation approach is suitable for use in the Chinese context. As highlighted in the discussion section, over time, we hope to apply a developmental evaluation approach (Patton, 2010) to health systems reform in China. Such a developmental approach is appropriate given that an incremental reform approach has been successfully applied for years in developing social innovations and promoting social changes (Xiao et al., 2013). We believe that a developmental evaluation approach applied over time can help build systematic understandings of requirements for innovation development in the complex process of the Chinese health system reform and development. This paper, however, confines its focus to describing the comprehensive indicator framework: over time, the evaluation team at CNHDRC will implement this framework in a variety of national and local contexts to learn about the impacts of health systems reform on health inequities in China.

A graphic framework informed by theories by Donabedian (1980), depicted in Figure 3.1, was developed to serve as a common ground for initial discussions. After careful studies of policy documents and rounds of consultations with five key health policymakers working in the NHFPC; four local

Figure 3.1. Conceptualizing Indicators Domains

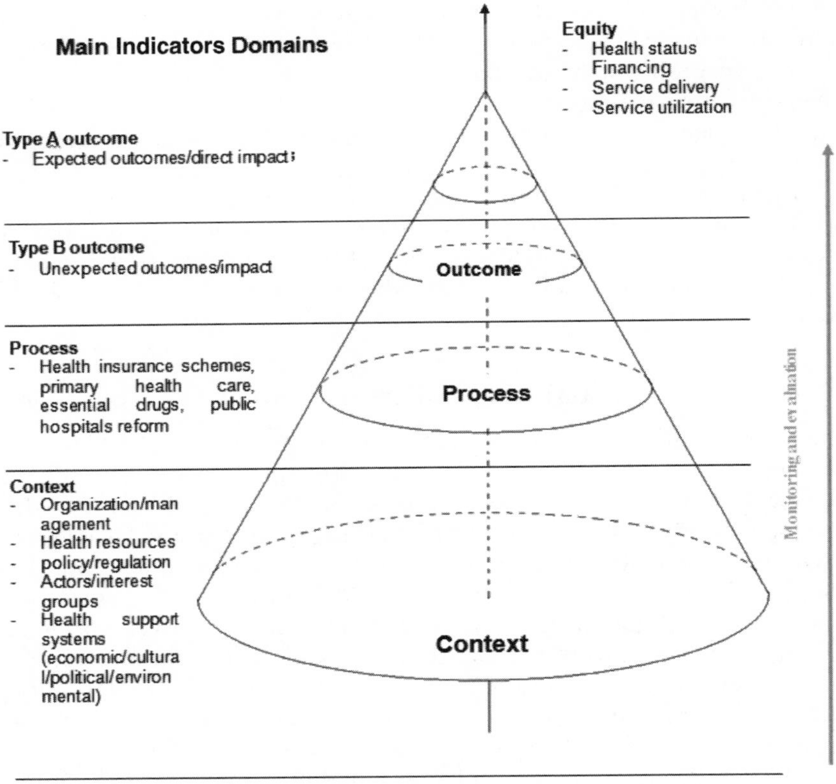

Main Indicators Domains

Equity
- Health status
- Financing
- Service delivery
- Service utilization

Type A outcome
- Expected outcomes/direct impacts

Type B outcome
- Unexpected outcomes/impact

Process
- Health insurance schemes, primary health care, essential drugs, public hospitals reform

Context
- Organization/management
- Health resources
- policy/regulation
- Actors/interest groups
- Health support systems (economic/cultural/political/environmental)

program implementers in Chongqing, Shaanxi, and Anhui provinces; and eight researchers and faculty members based in Beijing and local provinces, key questions for each indicator domain (Figure 3.2) were prepared.

In the 11th Five-Year Plan (2006–2010), the national government attached great importance to equity and social justice and embarked on preparation for universal health coverage. In the health plan issued in 2009, universal health coverage was formally proposed. As agreed by all policymakers and program implementers, equity was a fundamental value for health reforms and development during the 12th Five-Year Plan period (2011–2015). Gaps existed in life expectancy, maternal and child mortality in rural/urban areas, in different regions/provinces at different socioeconomic development levels and among population groups with different income level and residential status. Different financial protection schemes were designed for rural/urban patients and employed/unemployed patients, but in favor of patients with better affordability. Less capable rural health

Figure 3.2. Key Policy Questions Addressed

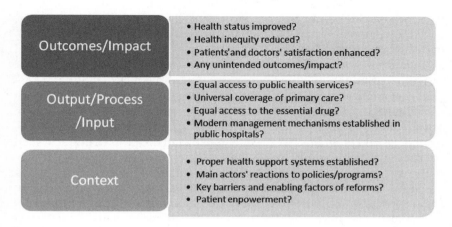

Outcomes/Impact
- Health status improved?
- Health inequity reduced?
- Patients'and doctors' satisfaction enhanced?
- Any unintended outcomes/impact?

Output/Process /Input
- Equal access to public health services?
- Universal coverage of primary care?
- Equal access to the essential drug?
- Modern management mechanisms established in public hospitals?

Context
- Proper health support systems established?
- Main actors' reactions to policies/programs?
- Key barriers and enabling factors of reforms?
- Patient enpowerment?

service delivery systems and poorly developed primary healthcare discouraged poor communities' access to essential health services.

The conceptual model is in iceberg shape with three indicator domains. Top of the iceberg is the outcome/impact domain, which is the part of most concern to key actors, such as policymakers and the population. There are two types of impacts: visible (short-or medium-term) impacts and unintended and long-term impacts. The former includes intended and immediate impacts, whereas the latter includes unintended impacts or impacts that would take a rather long time to show up. Although impacts occupy the tip of the iceberg for the sake of visualization of the model, it does not necessarily mean that this part is small or insignificant. On the contrary, outcome/impact is a critical aspect of the whole framework. As agreed by the policy stakeholders, the conceptual framework needed to pay attention to unexpected impacts of a health policy or public program and the process evaluation needed to explore processes/mechanisms underlying the unintended impacts.

The middle part of the model is the process domain, which mainly refers to the monitoring and evaluation of performance of health system reform and development. This part centers round key interventions, programs, projects, and tasks under the current health reform. A set of performance indicators will be generated and used to monitor and evaluate performance of the reform and health development plan. The Center for Health Statistics and Information (CHSI) of the Ministry of Health has been working on this part. It has developed a framework and put it into use to meet information needs of the health policymakers. Our process domain has tried to accommodate the current CHSI framework.

The lowest part is the context domain, referring to contextual or local information that will inform the monitoring and evaluation of health reform and development on national level or in a certain province. The context-specific information includes current status of health support systems, which can be categorized into political, social, cultural, economic, and environmental systems. Contextual questions will be explored, including whether Universal Health Coverage targets were included in the local economic and social development plan, the strength of the public finance system, distribution of ethnic minorities, and also issues of culture or customs that might shape the intervention. These systems have direct influence over the healthcare system. Actors/interest groups refer to those who are actively involved in or passively influenced by health reforms and development plans and programs. We need to understand their role in health system strengthening and politics and interests represented by them, which may influence health policy making and implementation. Information concerning health resources can provide us with the current status of the national health system or local health delivery system in terms of health infrastructure, human resources, and health funds. Organization/management refers to mechanisms or management systems guiding the national health system or local health delivery system.

To link the conceptual framework with current needs of the health system reform and strengthening, we mapped onto the framework the key questions posed by the central policymakers for the new round of health and development of the 12th Five-Year Plan for Health (see Figure 3.2), mainly concerning the outcomes and process domain. Two questions are added in the outcomes/impact part, which are about actors' satisfaction and unintended outcomes/impact of the health reform. We also developed questions for the context part based on our understanding of the system.

According to the key questions, we identified key indicator domains (see Figure 3.3). One key focus is the process indicator domain: this domain measures the "process as outcome" aspect of the health system. This part mainly concerns health system performance evaluation, namely performance of urban and rural healthcare delivery systems. Four indicator dimensions were chosen based on literature reviews, consultations and discussions with national health planners, health reformers, and decision makers at the division-chief level, namely access to basic quality health care, efficiency of health delivery systems, and health equity for all, with a focus on the differences between rural and urban health systems. Equity, as an axis dimension, cuts through all indicator domains, to reflect an important perspective of the Chinese health policymakers' current thinking behind health system strengthening.

Application of the Conceptual Indicators System

A detailed indicators framework for discussions was developed (Table 3.1) after consultations with policymakers and experts in relevant fields. The framework was used by the team in their proposal for setting up a national

Figure 3.3. A Framework of Indicator Domains

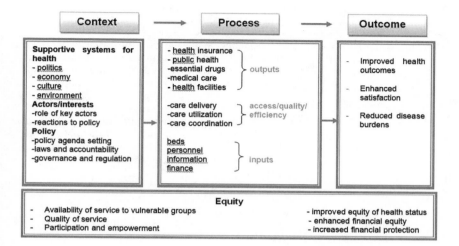

indicators system for evaluating the 12th Five-Year Plan for Health Reforms and Development (2011–2015) in September 2011. Discussions based on the framework were convened and feedback from policymakers obtained. The national health planners, health policy experts, and evaluators agreed that the indicator system for the national health plan should be embedded with an equity perspective and that contextual analysis was an important aspect of the evaluation of local health systems' performance.

After discussions with the health planners, the evaluators understood that they hoped to use monitoring and evaluation of the plan as a tool for holding central and provincial health policymakers and program implementers accountable. However, it is difficult to do so in a decentralized and fragmented health decision-making setting. As a compromise, they invited different departments to submit core indicators for inclusion in the process domain and required the CNHDRC researchers to work on the proposed indicators and complement them with necessary indicators.

As a way to move forward, the central health planners included all 24 indicators (Table 3.2) proposed by various departments in the NHFPC in the draft national health plan and asked the CNHDRC researchers to propose some other indicators that could capture progress and measure outcomes in accordance with the objectives and main priorities defined in the plan. The evaluators consulted with the relevant departments and policymakers on different indicators and finally 24 other indicators were listed for the 12th Five-Year Health Plan(Table 3.3).

The 24 supplementary indicators finally included were reflecting trade-offs of various end-users involved. Indicators were grouped in accordance with different departmental responsibilities. Some questions about specific

Table 3.1. Proposed Framework for Discussions

Indicator domain	Targets	Measurements	Equity perspective
Outcome/ impact	Improved health status of the population	Life expectancy	Regional/urban & rural
		Under-5 mortality rate	Regional/urban & rural/migrant and other vulnerable groups
		Maternal mortality rate	Regional/urban & rural/ migrant and other vulnerable groups
		Incidence and death rate of key infectious diseases	Regional/urban& rural/migrant and other vulnerable groups
		Prevalence and death rate of key non-communicable disease	Regional/urban& rural
		Incidence of birth defects	Regional/urban/migrant and other vulnerable groups
	Increased Satisfaction of Key Stakeholders	Doctors and patients'satisfaction for quality, efficiency, availability, reimbursement of health services	Provincial/urban & rural/migrant and other vulnerable groups
	Reduced Disease Burden	Ratio of catastrophic health expenditure	Provincial/urban & rural/migrant and other vulnerable groups
		Reduced incidence of disease-induced poverty	Provincial/urban & rural/migrant and other vulnerable groups
	Unintended Outcomes	Unexpected outcomes caused by implementation	Urban & rural/provincial/ vulnerable groups
Output/ process/ input	Improved Access to Primary Health Care and Health Protection	Universal coverage of and access to essential care (drugs, public health, medical services)	Provincial/urban & rural/migrant and other vulnerable groups
	Improved Care Quality/ Effectiveness	High-quality primary care, strengthened internal management of public hospitals, improved quality of care in secondary and tertiary hospitals	Provincial/urban & rural/migrant and other vulnerable groups
		Reduction of readmission and fatality rate	Provincial/urban & rural/migrant and other vulnerable groups

(Continued)

Table 3.1. Continued

Indicator domain	Targets	Measurements	Equity perspective
	Improved Health Efficiency	Institutional and systemwide efficiency, such as early interventions and shortened length of stay	Provincial/urban & rural/health facilities at different level
	Health Resources	Number of physicians, nurses, general practitioners (GPs), and other health personnel	Provincial/urban & rural
		Medical information systems	Provincial/urban & rural
		Health expenditures/public health inputs	Provincial/urban & rural
Context	Health Supportive Systems	Economic development, economic status of population groups	Provincial
		Hygienic rituals and customs, health awareness, and healthy behaviors	Provincial/urban & rural/minority/migrant and other vulnerable groups
		Health agenda setting process, health legislation, governance, and regulation	Provincial (municipal/county)
	Actors/ Relationship/ Interests	Main actors and their relationship with other formal or informal actors	-
		Actors'reactions to health reforms	-

interventions posed by the central health planners (Figure 3.2) were not addressed or inadequately covered, such as essential drugs and public hospitals reforms. Given the stress of the health system reform on vulnerable population's access to essential health services, the indicators system included equity as an important dimension for evaluation of the national health plan. Though context indicators were missing from the monitoring indicators, the health planners encouraged the evaluators to include them in the final evaluation by asking the local provinces to provide relevant data and information in their own evaluation reports.

Table 3.2. 24 Core Indicators for the 12th Five-Year Health Plan

Domains	Indicators
Health Outcomes	Life expectancy at birth
	Infant mortality
	Under-5 children mortality
	Maternal mortality
Disease Control and Prevention	Reporting rate of legal infectious diseases
	Number of living HIV/AIDS patients and carriers
	HBsAg+ population as percentage of the total population
	Coverage of national expanded programme on immunization at township level
	Awareness of major NCDs prevention and management
	Standard management of patients with hypertension
	Standard management of patients with diabetes
Maternal and Child Health	Management of under-3 children
	Coverage of prenatal care
	Coverage of hospital delivery
Health Inspection	Coverage of inspection of centralized water supply over 1,000 cubic meter per day
Financial Protection	Coverage of the New Rural Cooperative Scheme
	Payment ratio of listed items in the basic urban health insurance schemes
Medical Care	Average length of stay in tertiary hospitals
	Accordance rate of diagnosis at admission and discharge
Health Resources	Number of physicians per 1000 population
	Number of registered nurses per 1000 population
	Number of beds per 1000 population
Inputs	Share of per capita health expenditure in the total health expenditure
	Per capita fund for essential public health services

Conclusion

This chapter describes the attempts of developing a conceptual indicators framework for the Chinese health system strengthening in a short and medium term. A utilization-focused evaluation approach was taken to engage target users in framing key questions for evaluations and key components of an indicators system, so as to make the process more utilization focused. The conceptual framework proposed in the paper did serve as an initial platform for engaging end-users of evaluation of the 12th Five-Year National Health Plan in exploring and improving the indicators system.

For a country in rapid political, economic, and social transition, China has embarked on radical reforms in health sector in recent years. For the first time, the country decided to include evaluation as a mandate part in the national plan for health reforms and development. Facilitated by the evaluators, users of the evaluation—national health planners, policy and program designers and implementers—reviewed questions they would address by implementing the plan and discussed openly about what they hope to

Table 3.3. 24 Supplementary Indicators for the 12th Five-Year Health Plan

Domains	Indicators
Public Health System	Coverage of nucleic acid detection in blood banks
Medical Service System	Number of beds and service volume by private health facilities as a share of the total
	Share of rural patients seeking care within a county
Financial Protection	Reimbursement of outpatient care
	Per capita public finance for health
Public Health	Number of tuberculosis (TB) patients detected and treated
	Coverage of management of drug-resistant TB at city level
	Share of county (city, prefecture) without iodine deficiency disorders
	Share of communities and towns conducting blood sugar testing
	Coverage of health assessment of elderly at or over age 65
	Coverage of management of patients found with severe mental illness
	Coverage of care of patients found with severe mental illness
	Coverage of inspection of water quality in centralized water supply projects
	Screening coverage of common gynecologic disease
	Screening for neonatal inherited metabolic diseases
	Prevalence of growth retardation among under-5 children
	Prevalence of anemia among under-5 children
	Health literacy of urban and rural residents
	Smoking prevalence of people at age 15 or above
Medical Services	Blood donation
Health Personnel	Number of GPs trained
	GPs per 10,000 urban residents
	Share of township health centers with GPs
Information Systems	Coverage of standard digital health records

achieve with the evaluation of the plan. The deliberative process convened and organized, with help of the evaluators, created a space for various actors to hold dialogue and make changes. Although the indicators listed in the final 12th Five-Year National Health Plan were not fully based on the proposed indicator framework, the evaluators succeeded in bringing an utilization focus on evaluation.

Looking Forward

Looking forward, we think that the emerging evaluation community can contribute to enhancing health systems reform in China in the following ways:

- We do not see building a performance measurement as purely a conceptual or a data collection exercise. The challenge will be to develop the capacity to develop actions to act on this information. There are at least two critical questions as one builds on the conceptual foundation described in this chapter: What types of actions emerge from the collection and analysis of the data? What are the capacities and capabilities needed to "act" on the information from the performance measurement system described in this chapter?

- Much of the focus of the conceptual framework has been from a standardized monitoring perspective: for example, collecting standardized, uniform data across the multiple provinces of China to assess performance of the health system. One key challenge going forward is to explore how strategically planned evaluations can be linked to data from national-level surveys to assess progress of specific interventions in affecting health inequities. It may be hard to assess "what interventions works for whom" just through monitoring datasets. Rigorously designed evaluations that are also informed from a utilization perspective, might be needed to help learning about "what works for whom."
- There has also been an increased appreciation among Chinese policymakers that evaluations can serve very different purposes. As noted earlier, one evaluation approach that we plan to implement is the developmental evaluation approach (Patton, 2010). Many of the health system reform interventions are implemented in settings where the contextual features that inhibit or exacerbate inequities are not well understood. One of the strengths of the developmental approach is that the developmental evaluator works closely with the implementers of the intervention to help develop the implementation of the intervention in the specific contexts. Such a focus on developmental evaluation is relevant given both the complex dynamic realities of health system interventions and the heterogeneities of contexts in China and also the broader dynamic changes in the social, political, and economic conditions in China over the past few decades.
- China is a diverse country with spatial distribution in both health outcomes as well as in the social determinants of health. One critical challenge as we build on the performance indicators described in this chapter is how to incorporate knowledge of spatial heterogeneities into the evaluation and learning framework for the China Health System reform effort. It is also possible that the drivers of health inequities might vary across the regions and provinces of China. One of the challenges going forward will be to explore if there is a need for more specific "local" measures that are focused on the "local" drivers of health inequities, in addition to a uniform core of indicators that are collected across China.

References

Alva, S., Kleinau, E., Pomeroy, A., & Rowan, K. (2009). *Measuring the impact of health system strengthening: A review of the literature.* Washington, DC: U.S. Agency for International Development.

Centers for Disease Control and Prevention. (2016). A framework for Program Evaluation. https://www.cdc.gov/eval/framework/. Accessed on Feb. 24, 2016.

Donabedian, A. (1980). *The definition of quality and approaches to its assessment, Vol. 1: Explorations in quality assessment and monitoring*. Ann Arbor, MI: Health Administration Press.

Murray, C., & Frenk, J. (2000). A framework for assessing the performance of health systems. *Bulletin of the World Health Organization*, 78(6), 717–731.

Patton, M. Q. (2008). *Utilization-focused evaluation* (4th ed.). Thousand Oaks, CA: Sage Publications.

Patton, M. Q. (2010). Developmental evaluation: Applying complexity concepts to enhance innovation and use. New York: Guilford Press.

World Health Organization. (2000). *The World health report 2000*. Geneva: WHO.

Xiao, Y., Zhao, K., Bishai, D., & Peters, D. (2013). Essential drugs policy in three rural counties in China:What does a complexity lens add? *Social Science & Medicine, 93*, 220–228. https://doi.org/10.1016/j.socscimed.2012.09.034

Yip, W. C., Hsiao, W. C., Chen, W., Hu, S., Ma, J., & Maynard, A. (2012). Early appraisal of China's huge and complex health-care reforms. *Lancet, 379*(9818), 833–842. https://doi.org/10.1016/S0140-6736(11)61880-1

YUE XIAO *is a senior researcher at the China National Health Development Research Center in Beijing, China.*

KUN ZHAO *is a professor at the China National Health Development Research Center in Beijing, China.*

SANJEEVSRIDHARAN *is the director of The Evaluation Centre for Complex Health Interventions at St. Michael's Hospital and an associate professor with the Institute of Health Policy, Management and Evaluation at the University of Toronto in Canada.*

XIAOHONG CAO *is a researcher at the China National Health Development Research Center in Beijing, China.*

NEW DIRECTIONS FOR EVALUATION • DOI: 10.1002/ev

Yu, M., He, X., Hou, Y., & Li, X. (2017). Lessons learned from evaluating China's new cooperative medical scheme. In S. Sridharan, K. Zhao, & A. Nakaima (Eds.), *Building Capacities
to Evaluate Health Inequities: Some Lessons Learned from Evaluation Experiments in China,
India and Chile. New Directions for Evaluation, 154,* 55–64.

4

Lessons Learned from Evaluating China's New Cooperative Medical Scheme

Mo Yu, Xiaoyan He, Yunxin Hou, Xue Li

Abstract

*China's New Cooperative Medical Scheme (NCMS), established in 2003, is a
universal health care insurance program for rural residents aimed to improve
access to basic health care services and reduce financial risks of catastrophic illnesses in the rural population. It is a cornerstone of China's most recent health
care reform efforts. The purpose of this paper is to share insights and learnings from two evaluations of NCMS payment reform. The evaluations were conducted by local researchers and evaluators who were deeply involved in the design and implementation of NCMS in their own region and have gone through a
process of reflection of their own work to bring learnings to the broader health
systems and evaluation communities in China.* © 2017 Wiley Periodicals, Inc.,
and the American Evaluation Association.

In a country with a population of over 1.3 billion, ensuring access and
affordability of health care for every citizen is a major challenge. This
challenge is further complicated by the wide variation in geography,
socioeconomic status, culture, education, and disease burden in different
regions of the country. Approximately half of China's population resides
in rural areas, where on average, greater health inequities persist and access to health care is relatively limited compared to those residing in urban
centers (National Bureau of Statistics of China, 2015; Park, 2008). On average, rural residents tend to possess fewer social and economic means to

obtain the health care they need compared to their urban counterparts (Park, 2008). Since the 1980s, ensuring basic health care coverage for rural residents has been a top priority for the Chinese government. In 2003, the New Cooperative Medical Scheme (NCMS) was established, which is a universal health insurance program for rural residents aimed to improve access to basic health care services and reduce financial risks of catastrophic illnesses in the rural population (You & Kobayashi, 2009; Zhang, Yi, & Rozelle, 2010). The NCMS is a collaborative insurance program that receives funding subsidies from the central, provincial, and municipal governments and also requires small contributions (premiums) from rural residents. The NCMS is a cornerstone of China's health system reform efforts and plays a fundamental role in China's vision of achieving universal health care coverage (State Council, 2002).

In the last decade, commendable progress has been made in implementing the NCMS countrywide in terms of greatly increasing program coverage, participation, and funding level for reimbursement (Ulrich, Hoosain, & Kerins, 2011). The NCMS continues to evolve and adapt as it aims to provide better insurance coverage for China's rural population. However, NCMS still faces major challenges with regard to reducing patients' out-of-pocket expenditure, affecting patient-level outcomes, addressing health inequities across the country, and improving system efficiencies (Liang, Guo, Jin, Peng, & Zhang, 2012; Wagstaff, Lindelow, Gao, Xu, & Qian, 2009; Zhang, Cheng, Tolhurst, Tang, & Liu, 2010). To date, a large number of evaluations have been conducted to understand the impact of NCMS and to identify gaps and areas of improvement.

For the evaluation community, evaluating the NCMS is highly relevant because of the complex socioeconomic and political context in which the NCMS program operates and the multiple challenges faced by the program. China's health care reform is also bringing major changes to all aspects of the health care system. Consequently, the NCMS has to constantly adapt to meet the needs of the system and the population. Therefore, evaluating and learning from evaluations of a highly complex and dynamic program such as the NCMS can shed light on key insights for both the health systems and evaluation communities. Such insights and learnings can be also applied to other programs and settings and contribute to the growing field of evaluation in China.

The purpose of this paper is to present key learnings and reflections from two NCMS evaluations conducted in Shaanxi Province. The evaluations were conducted by local researchers and evaluators who were deeply involved in the design and implementation of NCMS in their own region. This paper is also a product of an international collaborative capacity-building project between the China National Health Development Research Center and the Evaluation Centre for Complex Health Interventions based in Toronto, Canada. Together, the project aimed to build capacity in evaluative thinking and evaluation skills among Chinese researchers and policymakers and build knowledge and skills around health equity evaluation (see Chapter 1 in this volume). The two evaluations presented here are the work of those who participated in the capacity-building project and serve to demonstrate the learnings and progress made by project participants. Key learnings and potential implications for the evaluation community are summarized.

Policy Background

In order to evaluate NCMS, it is important to understand the political and social context that gave birth to the program and the overall structure of the public health care system in China. In the late 1980s, major social and economic reforms swept across the nation. Under the leadership of Xiaoping Deng, China opened its gates to foreign investment and encouraged domestic entrepreneurism. Deng's promarket reforms encouraged decollectivization and privatization of traditionally state-owned and state-operated sectors, such as agriculture and health care. In order to promote economic growth, the central government directed funding away from health care into other sectors such as manufacturing and pulled away from its role as a payer of last resort for health care (Brown, Píriz, Liu, & Moore, 2012). As a result, government subsidies for public hospitals significantly decreased and public hospitals had to rely on user charges for a large proportion of their revenue in order to survive in market competition (Eggleston & Yip, 2004). Income from prescription drugs and high-technology diagnostic procedures has become a major source of revenue for hospitals, and hospitals have adopted practices such as drug price markup, overprescription and treatment, and prescription of expensive medications or high-tech diagnostic procedures in order to maximize revenue (Li et al., 2012; Wang, 2014). Such revenue-generating practices have led to increases in health care costs and unaffordability of health care in many rural areas (Yip & Hsiao, 2008). As a result, many rural residents became further impoverished due to their medical bills or simply refused health care because of unaffordability, leading to worsened health outcomes (Wagstaff, Lindelow, Wang, & Zhang, 2009). In recent years, progress has been made to change NCMS policies (for example, payment scheme) as an attempt to remove incentives for overprescription and to improve affordability of health care.

Zhen'an County NCMS Payment Method Reform Evaluation

The first evaluation focused on the reimbursement method reform for inpatient services in the NCMS program in Zhen'an County, Shaanxi Province, located in the northwest region of China. Zhen'an County is mostly composed of rural population, with a broad mix of ethnicities. The local NCMS program was established in 2003 with a fee-for-service payment model and unit prices set by the government. Under the fee-for-service payment model, physicians and hospitals are paid every time a service is provided. Therefore, payment is dependent on the quantity of services and not the quality of services. The fee-for-service payment model, combined with the increasing pressure on hospitals to self-sustain and a lack of proper supervision, provided incentives for hospitals to overprescribe and overtreat in order to maximize profit (Li, et al., 2012; Wang, 2014). In order to address this issue, Zhen'an County carried out a payment method reform for the NCMS, replacing the fee-for-service model with the case payment model and per-diem payment model. In case payment, one standard payment is made for every case or discharge, regardless of the actual cost of care. In per diem payment, a standard fee is charged on a per bed-day basis. Both payment methods attempted to remove incentives for overprescription and overtreatment. The payment reform was carried out in 2010 and an evaluation was done subsequently.

This evaluation highlights several key learnings that are salient for Chinese policymakers. First, recognizing the interdependencies between the intervention and the policy context in which it operates is critical for understanding and evaluating the intervention. In this evaluation, the goals of the NCMS payment reform are potentially in conflict with the structure of the public hospital system in China. After the payment reform that replaced fee-for-service with case payment and per-diem payment, the new payment models removed incentives for overprescription and overtreatment, as hospitals received the same amount of payment regardless of the quantity of medications prescribed or services provided. In other words, hospitals could no longer profit from overprescription and overtreatment due to the constraints imposed by the new payment system. As a result, there was a significant reduction in inpatient health care costs and in hospital revenues, and a major source of the hospitals' income was eliminated. However, the hospitals are not being compensated for the loss of income and were still required to sustain themselves with minimal subsidies from the government. Most hospitals reported dissatisfaction with the compensation they received and the new payment rates being too low. This raises a long-term sustainability issue. Without being properly compensated, the hospitals faced enormous challenges with the new payment scheme because they could not generate enough revenue to sustain normal operation. Therefore, incentives need to incorporate ideas of sustainability. Aligning financial incentives with provider performance and basing performance measures on evidence of treatment effectiveness could substantially improve health care quality and efficiency. The key question is how to measure and estimate a proper compensation amount to balance the different needs of stakeholders. In the case of Zhen'an county, the reform did temporarily reduce inpatient costs but potentially created a system that was unsustainable. The notion of sustainable impacts is an underresearched area of evaluation; however, it is critical for evaluating health systems reform interventions, given the nature of and the long timelines involved in the process.

New Directions for Evaluation • DOI: 10.1002/ev

The second key learning is about understanding the timeline of impact of a given intervention to manage expectations and correctly interpret evaluation results. Often, the timeframe of an evaluation is quite short. Policymakers would like to know the outcomes of the program and whether it worked sooner rather than later. However, such questions often take time to answer. Each program has its own mechanism and trajectory of impact. Unlike simple interventions, complex interventions have many factors in play and changes may take place much faster or slower than we anticipate (Sridharan & Nakaima, 2010). Changes may take place in different forms than we anticipate and may cause rippling effects of downstream changes. In the case of NCMS, evaluators and policymakers must be cognizant of the complex processes involved in pushing through a system-level change, which has major ramifications for all parts of the system. We also have to be aware of the possible reactions from different system players, both internal and external. A comprehensive understanding of the factors that could influence the outcomes of the intervention could help to correctly interpret evaluation results, set realistic and meaningful timelines of impact, and properly manage stakeholder expectations.

Milstein et al. (2007, p. 6) recommended the use of formal system dynamic modeling procedures to understand the anticipated performance trajectories of key outcomes for programs: "Popular conceptions about how certain phenomena change over time may often fail to account for real-world sources of inertia and delay and may suggest that things can change more rapidly than is actually possible." Thus, it is important to understand and communicate to policymakers that if evaluation finds a program unsuccessful in reaching policy targets, it may be that we are expecting changes too soon. Changes in complex interventions might take time. As noted by Woolcock (2009), evaluators must have some initial ideas of the anticipated trajectory of impact of a program in order to select the best time point to evaluate it.

Hanbin District NCMS Payment Method Reform Evaluation

The second evaluation also looked at NCMS payment reform and took place in the Hanbin District of Shaanxi Province. In 2010, Hanbin District launched a reform of NCMS payment methods, replacing the fee-for-service with prospective payment with a global budget for outpatient care and mixed payment methods for inpatient care. In the global budget model, the health facility receives a lump sum to cover all specified services during a given period. At the end of the period, the hospital keeps any surpluses and covers any shortfalls. In the mixed payment methods, different payment methods were used depending on the disease type, including case payment, per-diem payment, and fee-for-service payment. In 2010, the global budget payment scheme for outpatient care was implemented in 45 township health centers (THCs) and the mixed payment method was implemented in one secondary hospital and 10 THCs. An evaluation of the payment reform was conducted to understand its impact on medical cost and provider behavior change by collecting quantitative financial information and inpatient and outpatient visit records and conducting semistructured key informant interviews with hospital management, physicians, and patients.

The first key learning from this evaluation concerns the idea of preconceived bias. Evaluations have always been challenged by different stakeholders with a variety of interests. On the one hand, active involvement of stakeholders can encourage them to offer dissenting opinions or alternative perspectives to ensure the objectivity of evaluations. It is also beneficial to place the evaluation in its policy context for it to be valid, relevant, and useful (Markiewicz, 2008). On the other hand, conflicts of interest between evaluators and stakeholders often result in political pressures that jeopardize the independence and objectivity of the evaluations. In such complex environments with multiple interest groups, it would require exceptional judgment, responsibility, and wisdom to produce a credible evaluation. Within the context of politics, evaluations require careful consideration not only of the evaluation itself but also of the larger political structure into which it is expected to fit.

In China's case, the effectiveness and sustainability of NCMS carry great political significance for the Chinese government. As a central piece underlying the health care reform and China's commitment to universal health care coverage, there is pressure to ensure the success of the NCMS. Such pressure disseminates and manifests itself among implementers and evaluators of the NCMS, who may have formed preconceived ideas and attitudes about their programs before they even began their work. They may believe that the program will surely be and has to be a success. Consequently, during the process of evaluation, the implementer and evaluator may pay attention only to positive evidence while ignoring negative ones. Such mentality can influence each stage of the evaluation process but is particularly highlighted during the formulation of evaluation findings or recommendations (Markiewicz, 2008). Such preconceived biases can affect evaluators' ability to evaluate programs objectively and provide useful recommendations. As a result, program evaluations may be inaccurate and many underlying problems may be overlooked, hindering the development and reform of the health system in the long run.

From a broader point of view, a culture of evidence-based decision making is relatively new and has not been fully established in China. Evaluation is a new area for Chinese practitioners in different fields and for a long time was misunderstood to be the same as monitoring or regulation. Because of the lack of systematic training in evaluation theories and methods, practitioners or evaluators have not fully recognized the usefulness of evaluation, especially how evaluations can help policy stakeholders learn. Therefore, the preconceived biases can also result from a lack of knowledge of evaluation theories and design and not knowing how to conduct proper

New Directions for Evaluation • DOI: 10.1002/ev

evaluations. Local NCMS managers and evaluators may not know how to determine if the evaluation design is sound, the evaluation method is proper, and results are reliable, due to a lack of systematic training and study of research methodologies. Thus, they are more likely to rely on pre-conceived biases and perhaps sometimes draw unscientific conclusions.

The second point concerns the use of proxy measures to evaluate outcomes in the absence of actual information on desired outcomes. The use of patient satisfaction measures is a good example. In NCMS evaluations, patient satisfaction measures are often used as an indicator for the success of the program and as an important piece of information to inform decision making. Such practice is often based on the assumption that higher satisfaction equals higher quality care, which in turn leads to better outcomes. However, in reality, because of many factors such as culture, socioeconomic status, personal inclinations, baseline physical health, mental health, and survey methods, patient satisfaction measures may not accurately reflect the quality of care received or any meaningful changes in health outcomes. According to Bleich, Ozaltin, and Murray (2009), patient experience is an important determinant of satisfaction with the health system but it explains only about 10% of its variation. The majority (90%) of the variation is explained by factors that are unrelated to patient experience such as patient expectations, self-reported health status, and personality. Bleich et al. also suggested the role of other social factors external to the health system that possibly shape patients' satisfaction with the health system. Factors such as the portrayal of the health care system by the media, the discussion of the system by political leaders, or important national events such as war or the performance of national football teams may be partly responsible for the remaining variation in satisfaction with the health care system. Thus, measuring satisfaction with a health system by patient experience may be an oversimplification of the impacts of an intervention. Because of this over-simplified nature of the satisfaction studies, they often yield results that do not accurately reflect the true progress of the programs.

In the evaluation of payment reform in Hanbin, patient satisfaction with cost reduction and health care outcomes was used as indicators. Two questions were asked: "Are you satisfied with medical costs?" and "Are you satisfied with outcomes of the health care you received?" Results showed that the majority of patients were satisfied with cost reductions, but a large number of patients were not satisfied with the outcomes. Two reasons were identified. First, after eliminating the fee-for-service payment scheme, doctors tended not to overprescribe or prescribe new or advanced drugs because there is now less incentive to do so. Second, doctors also reduced the use of intravenous injections, antibiotics, hormones, and other services as required by the payment reform. These changes in practice are necessary to reduce improper behaviors on the providers' part and to reduce unnecessary medical costs. However, from a patient's point of view, these changes are easily mistaken as reductions in health care quality. For one thing, patients are not getting as many services as they did before. For another, patients with a severe cold, for example, may recover at a slower rate than before due to the lower doses of antibiotics used. All these factors can contribute to lower satisfaction with health care outcome.

Multiple mechanisms need to be considered on why changes in satisfaction might not accurately measure program impacts. One potentially important mechanism is the information asymmetry between patients and health providers. Physicians are trained and qualified to make certain medical decisions that the patients are not, but patients may not always agree with the physician's recommendations. The services deemed appropriate by physicians may not always be in line with what the patients expect to receive. There is an adaptive process to achieve the consensus between the patients' expectation and the appropriate services defined by physicians. The common goals on both sides is to provide effective and affordable health services to patients. This example highlights the importance of selecting and aligning indicators with the objectives of the intervention. Changes on the system level take time and using the wrong indicators can be misleading. Proper indicator selection is a key step for program evaluation. Furthermore, monitoring of indicators should be integrated with evaluation and infused with evaluative thinking in order to meaningfully inform program decisions or policies.

Conclusion

This paper presented two examples of evaluations done by local practitioners working on China's health system reform. Valuable lessons learned and insights from the evaluations include the importance of recognizing interdependencies between the intervention and its policy context; understanding an intervention's trajectory of impact to manage expectations and accurately interpret evaluation results; selecting indicators that properly align with objectives of the intervention; and empowering evaluators with the knowledge, judgment, and skills to maintain objectivity in highly political contexts. These learnings are valuable not only to Chinese evaluators working on NCMS but also to other health system reform interventions and to the broader evaluation community. The evaluations also highlight a need to build a more reflective culture of evaluation, one focused on learning and development.

References

Bleich, S., Ozaltin, E., & Murray, C. (2009). How does satisfaction with the health-care system relate to patient experience? *Bulletin of the World Health Organization, 87,* 271–278.

Brown, R., Píriz, D., Liu, Y., & Moore, J. (2012). *Reforming health care in China: Historical, economic and comparative perspectives* (Pubpol 716). Ann Arbor, MI: University of Michigan, Gerald R. Ford School of Public Policy.

Eggleston, K., & Yip, W. (2004). Hospital competition under regulated prices: Application to urban health sector reforms in China. *International Journal of Health Care Finance and Economics, 4*(4), 343–368.

Li, Y., Xu, J., Wang, F., Wang, B., Liu, L., Hou, W., ... Lu, Z. (2012). Overprescribing in China, driven by financial incentives, results in very high use of antibiotics, injections, and corticosteroids. *Health Affairs (Millwood), 31*(5), 1075–1082.

Liang, X., Guo, H., Jin, C., Peng, X., & Zhang, X. (2012). The effect of New Cooperative Medical Scheme on health outcomes and alleviating catastrophic health expenditure in China: A systematic review. *PLoS ONE, 7*(8), e40850.

Markiewicz, A. (2008). The political context of evaluation: What does this mean for independence and objectivity? *Evaluation Journal of Australasia, 8*(2), 35–41.

Milstein, B., Jones, A., Homer, J., Murphy, D., Essien, J., & Seville, D. (2007). Charting plausible futures for diabetes prevalence in the United States: A role for system dynamics simulation modeling. *Preventing Chronic Disease, 4*(3).

National Bureau of Statistics of China. (2015). *China statistical yearbook*. Beijing, China: China Statistics Press.

Park, A. (2008). Chapter 2: Rural-urban inequality in China. In S. Yusuf, & T. Saich (Eds.), *China Urbanizes: Consequences, Strategies and Policies* (pp. 41–63). Washington, DC: World Bank.

Sridharan, S., & Nakaima, A. (2010). Ten steps to making evaluation matter. *Evaluation and Program Planning, 34*(2), 135–146.

State Council. (2002). *Decisions of the State Council on strengthening rural healthcare*. Beijing, China: State Council.

Ulrich, J., Hoosain, A., & Kerins, H. (2011). *Medicine for the masses—China's healthcare reform: Progress and future steps.* J. P. Morgan.

Wagstaff, A., Lindelow, M., Gao, J., Xu, L., & Qian, J. (2009). Extending health insurance to the rural population: An impact evaluation of China's new cooperative medical scheme. *Journal of Health Economics, 28*(1), 1–19.

Wagstaff, A., Lindelow, M., Wang, S., & Zhang, S. (2009). *Reforming China's rural health system.* Washington, DC: World Bank.

Wang, Y. (2014). The issue of over-prescription: Drug prescription relating to the government power in China. *Cambridge Journal of China Studies, 9*(3).

Woolcock, M. (2009). Toward a plurality of methods in project evaluation: a contextualised approach to understanding impact trajectories and efficacy. *Journal of Development Effectiveness, 1*(1), 1–14.

Yip, W., & Hsiao, W. (2008). The Chinese health system at a crossroads. *Health Affairs, 27*(2), 460–468.

You, X., & Kobayashi, Y. (2009). The New Cooperative Medical Scheme in China. *Health Policy, 91*(1), 1–9.

Zhang, L., Cheng, X., Tolhurst, R., Tang, S., & Liu, X. (2010). How effectively can the New Cooperative Medical Scheme reduce catastrophic health expenditure for the poor and non-poor in rural China? *Tropical Medicine & International Health, 15*(4), 468–475.

Zhang, L., Yi, H., & Rozelle, S. (2010). Good and bad news from China's New Cooperative Medical Scheme. *IDS Bulletin, 41*(4), 95–106.

MO YU *is a research coordinator at the Evaluation Centre for Complex Health Interventions at St. Michael's Hospital in Canada.*

XIAOYAN HE *is deputy director of NCMS Administrative Center in Zhen'an county Shaanxi Province in China.*

YUNXIN HOU is Director General of the Institute of Health Promotion in Hanbin district in Shaanxi Province in China

XUE LI is a researcher based at the China National Health Development Research Center in Beijing, China.

NEW DIRECTIONS FOR EVALUATION • DOI: 10.1002/ev

Sridharan, S., Zhao, K., Nakaima, A., Maplazi, J., Yu, M., & Qiu, Y. (2017). Toward a structured process to evaluate health inequities: Lessons learned from developing and implementing evaluation guidelines to address health inequities. In S. Sridharan, K. Zhao, & A. Nakaima (Eds.), *Building Capacities to Evaluate Health Inequities: Some Lessons Learned from Evaluation Experiments in China, India and Chile*. New Directions for Evaluation, 154, 65–78.

5

Toward a Structured Process to Evaluate Health Inequities: Lessons Learned from Developing and Implementing Evaluation Guidelines to Address Health Inequities

Sanjeev Sridharan, Kun Zhao, April Nakaima, Joanna Maplazi, Mo Yu, Yingpeng Qiu

Abstract

This paper discusses the development and implementation of structured guidelines that contained a fixed set of questions as part of a project in building evaluation capacity for addressing health inequities in the health sector in China. The ambition of the guidelines was to test whether a structured process of questions could aid teams that did not have a strong background in evaluation to complete equity-focused evaluations and also help raise the salience of health equity as an important goal of health systems reform among the participants of the project. The guidelines were informed by multiple perspectives that included the literature on social determinants of health, realist evaluation, and utilization/influence perspectives. One noteworthy aspect of this project was that the participants in this capacity-building project were local and national policymakers, practitioners, and university researchers. Our original goal was to test these guidelines in equity-focused policy interventions in three separate provinces of China. One key insight from this project was that there is a need to move away from a testing perspective to a developmental approach in formulating evaluation guidelines that can work across multiple organizational and country contexts and also closely reflect the needs of practitioners and

I n her 2006 essay titled, "State of the Art in Research on Equity in Health," Barbara Starfield wrote: "Despite the very large research literature on social determinants of health, relatively little has been written that would inform the choice among policy alternatives to address inequities" (p. 14). Making decisions between policy alternatives to address inequities requires a culture of evaluation in policy settings. It requires thinking explicitly about addressing inequities as a policy goal. It also requires evaluation capacity within policy organizations to help make decisions between competing policy alternatives.

The government of China embarked on an ambitious process of health system reform in 2009. A key goal of the health system reform was to reduce health inequities especially between the urban and rural areas of China. As part of its vision of implementing health system reform, the government wanted to build capacities within the health sector to evaluate policies on a number of dimensions including equities.

As part of evaluation capacity-building efforts, the China National Health Development Research Center (CNHDRC) led the development of a project titled "Building Health Equity in China Through Evaluation Capacity Building" in partnership with two Canadian organizations, the International Development Research Centre and The Evaluation Centre for Complex Health Interventions (TECCHI) based in Toronto, Canada. CNHDRC is a national think tank that provides technical consultancy to health policymakers. It was set up in 1991 under the leadership of the National Health and Family Planning Commission. As part of this project, three teams based in three Chinese provinces conducted equity evaluations. The three local teams in China each included multiple researchers (often from local universities) and local policymakers and researchers from CNHDRC.

The evaluation guidelines are a series of structured questions that were intended to help complete an evaluation of equity projects and promote evaluation reflection. The guidelines were aligned very closely to the program of evaluation capacity building for evaluating health inequities (described in Chapter 1 of this volume). Figure 5.1 describes the theory of change (see Chapter 2 for details of the theory of change). As described in Chapter 1, a series of workshops/classes were also implemented to aid the completion of the evaluation guidelines.

The policy aspiration of research leaders at CNHDRC was to arrive at a tool composed of a set of questions that evaluation teams interested in health equities would need to address. Given the ambitious scope of the health system reform efforts in China, there was a desire to disseminate such a tool widely so that evaluative thinking about reducing inequities could be more widespread. One original goal of the project was to develop

Figure 5.1. Theory of Change of the Project

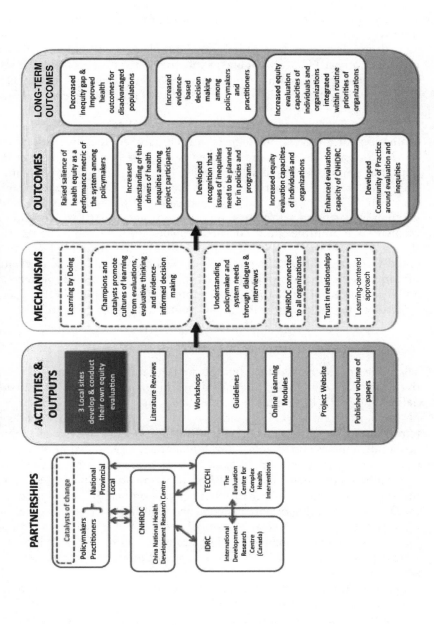

these guidelines and then empirically test them in the three policy projects that were being evaluated as part of the capacity-building project. The hope was that the three projects would serve as a test bed that would serve both as a measure of the utility of the guidelines as well as elicit ideas for further improvement.

Although a number of guidelines and tools exist in a number of areas in evaluation, we believe what makes this structured process is unique is its explicit focus on an accompanying curriculum on evaluating inequities and also in consideration of the structures needed to support the completion of the guidelines.

This paper addresses a simple question: Can the process of conducting evaluations of interventions focused on reducing equities be distilled to a few key questions? As the project itself is ongoing, we do not answer this question summatively but discuss what we have learned from implementing such a structured process in the China policy setting. The longer term ambition with the development and implementation of the guidelines was to test whether a structured set of questions could be generalized widely and implemented in multiple equity-focused projects in China. We recognize that this is an ambitious goal because it is unlikely that structured questions could work in a variety of situations. However, given the scope of evaluation involved in the health system reform both at the national, provincial, and local levels in China, there was an interest in exploring whether such a structured process could facilitate the completion of the evaluations.

Influences on Guidelines

The guidelines were informed by a Social Determinants of Health perspective (Solar & Irwin, 2010). The World Health Organization (WHO, 2016b) defines the Social Determinants of Health as "the conditions in which people are born, grow, work, live, and age, and the wider set of forces and systems shaping the conditions of daily life. These forces and systems include economic policies and systems, development agendas, social norms, social policies and political systems" (para. 1). WHO's Commission on the Social Determinants of Health (CSDH, 2008) recommends: "Creating the organizational space and capacity to act effectively on health inequity requires investment in training of policymakers and health practitioners and public understanding of social determinants of health. It also requires a stronger focus on social determinants in public health research" (p. 2). This project sought to train policymakers and health practitioners within an evaluation setting to focus on the social determinants of health in order to probe the barriers and unmet needs within each of the local areas and locate the policy interventions within the context of inequities.

Both the guidelines and the underlying structured processes were informed by a realist evaluation (Pawson, 2013) and a utilization/influence perspective (Mark & Henry, 2004; Patton, 2008). Realist evaluations focus on the context and mechanisms underlying outcomes. Following a realist perspective, the guidelines were intended to promote greater reflection around the distribution around the social determinants of health (Graham, 2004) and the mechanisms by which the interventions could disrupt patterns of inequities and the types of progress that can be anticipated across different contexts.

Much of the literature on inequities emphasizes the "problem space" of inequities: for example, the distributions of health gradients across levels of socioeconomic status. The literature on a knowledge base of solutions that work to address inequities across a variety of contexts is more limited. Following Tannahill and Sridharan (2013), we found distinctions between the "problem space" and "solution space" of health inequities and the use of evaluation as a "bridge" between the problem space and the solution space, a useful conceptualization to help guide the evaluation. By this, we mean that the evaluations needed to help understand the mechanisms and the underlying contexts that were generating inequities and also empirically explain how the intervention ("the solution") addresses the gradients in inequities.

Process of Developing Guidelines

The guidelines were developed through an iterative process. Three reviews of evaluations of health equity were completed. The first review treated equity interventions as complex systems (Pawson, 2013). The review helped highlight the reporting requirements for evaluations of equity interventions from a complexity lens: the review helped develop understanding of reporting standards for equity interventions that would help in the replication of interventions in different contextual settings. A second review focused on exemplary health equity evaluations from evaluation design perspectives. The emphasis of this review was on the methodological features of such exemplars, including how different articles explored threats to internal and external validity, the types of statistical models that were developed, and how statistical approaches to inequities were integrated with qualitative approaches. A third review explored the evaluations of the New Cooperative Medical Scheme (Liang, Guo, Jin, Peng, & Zhang, 2012; see Chapter 4 in this volume); this is the most rigorously evaluated health equity intervention in China. We explored the different types of learnings that are possible from the multiple evaluations and how such learnings can influence health equity policies and practice. This review was in part inspired by the evaluation influence framework developed by Mel Mark and Gary Henry (Mark & Henry, 2004).

The guidelines were also informed by dialogue with national and provincial policymakers in China on the types of evaluation questions that they would want the equity-focused evaluation to address (some of their feedback is discussed in Chapter 6). Based on the reviews and dialogue, an initial draft of the guidelines was developed.

As part of this project, TECCHI also conducted an evaluation school on evaluating inequities in Toronto, Canada. Participants in the school provided feedback on the original version of the guidelines. Additionally, leading research experts in health equity in Canada and China also provided feedback on the initial set of guidelines. An interim version of the guidelines that incorporated the feedback was then developed.

The Key Dimensions of the Health Equity Guidelines

Figure 5.2 describes the eight sections of the guidelines. Space considerations prevented us from discussing the guidelines in great detail; however, some of the key points of the developed guidelines are highlighted. The guidelines were intricately linked to the multiple workshops (see discussions by Zhao et al., Chapter 1 in this volume).

The "Problem Space" of Equity

Health inequities can be defined as "differences in health outcomes that are avoidable, unfair, and systematically related to social inequality and disadvantage" (Gardner, 2008, p. 4). Some differences in health outcomes between different subpopulations do not constitute health inequality—for example, older adults will normally have poorer dimensions of health than younger adults simply because of normal aging or genetic/biological factors that make some groups more prone to certain health risks/diseases. So when unequal health outcomes between different subpopulations are detected, analysis is needed to determine whether the observed "gap" is caused or exacerbated by a set of systematic socioeconomic or geographical factors.

The starting point in developing the evaluation was to think of the nature of the baseline inequity gap. Health inequity problems can be thought of as falling into one or several of the following categories: access (difficulty getting to services or not allowed services), affordability (services that are financially out of reach), availability (not enough service provided), quality (poor quality or perception of poor quality deters people from seeking services), uptake or use (services available and affordable but people are not using services; this could be because of differences in cultural norms, lack of awareness, perceptions of risk, etc.), or differential effectiveness (services do not help as much for a specific subpopulation, thus putting them at an added disadvantage). These categories and the scope of the problem are intended to help users of the guidelines to identify the focus of the evaluation. As part of this initial step, teams reflected on the nature of the inequity gap: whether the inequity gap was a problem of access, affordability, availability, quality, uptake or use, or differential effectiveness.

We also encouraged the teams to define what the baseline health gradient of inequity was before the start of the intervention. A health gradient

Figure 5.2. Components of the Guidelines

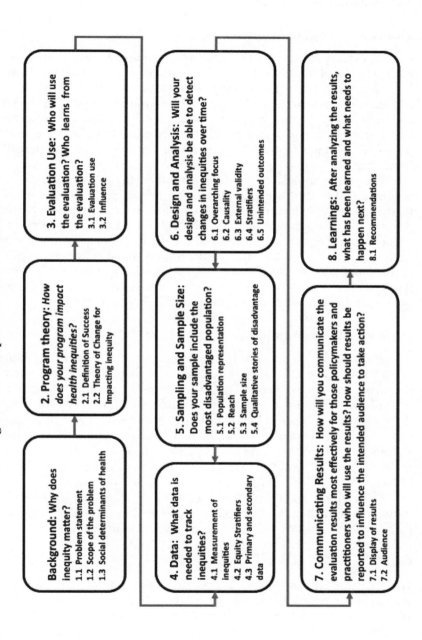

Background: Why does inequity matter?
1.1 Problem statement
1.2 Scope of the problem
1.3 Social determinants of health

2. Program theory: *How does your program impact health inequities?*
2.1 Definition of Success
2.2 Theory of Change for Impacting inequity

3. Evaluation Use: Who will use the evaluation? Who learns from the evaluation?
3.1 Evaluation use
3.2 Influence

4. Data: What data is needed to track inequities?
4.1 Measurement of inequities
4.2 Equity Stratifiers
4.3 Primary and secondary data

5. Sampling and Sample Size: Does your sample include the most disadvantaged population?
5.1 Population representation
5.2 Reach
5.3 Sample size
5.4 Qualitative stories of disadvantage

6. Design and Analysis: Will your design and analysis be able to detect changes in inequities over time?
6.1 Overarching focus
6.2 Causality
6.3 External validity
6.4 Stratifiers
6.5 Unintended outcomes

7. Communicating Results: How will you communicate the evaluation results most effectively for those policymakers and practitioners who will use the results? How should results be reported to influence the intended audience to take action?
7.1 Display of results
7.2 Audience

8. Learnings: After analyzing the results, what has been learned and what needs to happen next?
8.1 Recommendations

measures the distribution of health outcomes usually along a dimension of social determinant of health.

Theory of Change of Inequities

As the next step, the evaluation teams were required to define what success of the intervention (in terms of addressing inequities) meant for them and how the intervention would address inequities. In our experience, there is often not a clear understanding of the pathways by which interventions seek to reduce the inequity gap. Thinking explicitly about the pathways by which intervention activities could affect inequities can help the program planners and implementers develop the intervention so that it is more likely to succeed.

The guidelines also raised questions about the role of local social determinants of health that might influence the inequity gap. As part of the theory of change of inequities, we encouraged the participants to reflect on how the intervention proposed to address the multiple, intersecting causes of inequities. For example, as part of the theory of inequities, the evaluation needed to discuss how the intervention planned to address any of the problems of access, affordability, availability, quality, uptake/use, and differential effectiveness. We also encouraged the teams to reflect on how the intervention could affect the health gradient over time.

Evaluation Use and Influence

As noted earlier, the guidelines were informed by utilization and influence perspectives. Given that the evaluations were planned in a policy setting, we encouraged each of the evaluation teams to explore how the evaluations were planned to be used, who are the specific stakeholders planning to use the evaluation and needed to be influenced, and what types of evaluation questions relating to inequities would policymakers or practitioners want to address. Following Mark and Henry (2004), the workshops also discussed multiple mechanisms of individual, interpersonal, and collective levels of influence by which evaluations could influence stakeholders.

As noted earlier, a critical part of thinking about evaluation use and influence was to identify stakeholders who were key factors in the influence pathway that linked the learnings from evaluation to action.

Data

This step focused on being explicit about the data needed for measuring inequities over time, social and geographical equity stratifiers (WHO, 2016a), and the sources of primary and secondary data. Additionally, the workshop linked to this section of the guidelines discussed multiple measures of inequities and how changes in inequities would be measured over time. A range of equity measures (such as the Gini coefficient) were introduced in the capacity-building workshop. We encouraged the participants to connect the data needed with the theory of change of inequities.

Sampling and Sample Size

This step included reflection on whether the sampling strategy for the primary data would include individuals who were "hard to reach," bias in secondary data sources, and sample size and sampling for qualitative longitudinal evaluations. In the workshops, we encouraged a mixed methods approach in which primary data needed to be collected to complement the secondary sources of information. Further we stressed that the sampling needed to be informed by the theory of change of inequities.

We also paid attention to issues of sampling that required reaching hard-to-reach individuals or populations. As example, there has been a recent interest in developing innovation methods of sampling such as respondent-driven sampling (Johnston & Sabin, 2010) and time–space sampling to access individuals who are hard to reach. We encouraged a focus on sampling methods that would allow the primary data collection to capture experiences directly from individuals who are likely to experience multiple disadvantages and also hard to access.

As part of this step, the evaluation teams were required to explore whether secondary sources of data (e.g., administrative data) included information on individuals who were systematically disadvantaged. Missing data are an especially serious problem in equity research, and it was important that administrative data be used with care.

From a realist evaluation perspective, we encouraged greater attention to be paid to issues of context and mechanisms and the role of context in both the generation of inequities and in the potential success of the intervention.

As part of a mixed methods strategy, we also encouraged teams to follow a small sample of individuals and collect information qualitatively over time. This step could potentially help identify and describe stories of disadvantage and how individuals with multiple disadvantages benefited from the intervention or uncover barriers that had not been sufficiently addressed by the intervention.

Design and Analysis

The guidelines also encouraged a focus on design to explore whether changes in inequities over the course of the intervention could be attributed to the intervention. Design was introduced as a response to fairly well established ideas of threats to internal and external validity. Additionally we sought at the design stage to clarify how some of the key assumptions in the theories of change could be tested empirically.

The guidelines encouraged analysis of impacts on a variety of equity dimensions including access, affordability, quality, uptake/use, and differential effectiveness. As part of the design step, both intended and unintended impacts of the program were stressed. Following a realist evaluation approach, we encouraged the teams to explore the mechanisms that might explain the intended and unintended impacts. The analysis methods that were taught encouraged both univariate and multivariate ways of assessing changes in equities over time and also how qualitative and quantitative methods could be integrated to test key assumptions of the theory of inequities. For example, one mixed methodology design discussed in the workshop was how multilevel models could be integrated with qualitative longitudinal research methods help in exploring contexts, mechanisms, and outcomes associated with inequities. The evaluation teams were encouraged to think of heterogeneous impacts of the intervention across different social determinants of health. The classic realist evaluation mantra of "what works for whom and under what circumstances" was especially relevant from an inequities perspective; the analytical focus was on differential effectiveness of programs for different subgroups of individuals.

Communication

A critical focus of the project was to encourage each of the local teams to communicate the learnings and results of the evaluation on an ongoing basis. Each of the evaluation teams were encouraged to develop policy-friendly graphics that highlighted the heterogeneous impacts of the intervention. Additionally, teams were also encouraged to have their communication and dissemination efforts be guided by understandings of the evaluation influence framework discussed at the evaluation use and influence step. We encouraged targeted communication focused on such key stakeholders.

Learnings

In this final step, teams were encouraged to reflect on what they had learned about inequities, the types of inequity-specific recommendations they would make as a result of the evaluation, and how the evaluation shed further light on the theory of inequities. We also encouraged reflections on how the policy, practice, or implementation needed to be redesigned based on learnings from an inequity perspective. In the workshops, we stressed that the shift from findings to recommendations is almost never straightforward: understanding of the policy landscape is important in moving toward recommendations.

Lessons Learned: Lessons in Humility

We describe lessons learned from the projects to improve the guidelines and also to make such guidelines more salient for future evaluations of health equity initiatives.

Key lessons learned included:

1. *The guidelines might not be the "active ingredient" of learning*: A key learning was that perhaps the original vision of creating a tool composed of a structured set of questions that could generate higher quality equity evaluations was too ambitious. Our learning over the course of this project was that it was not the list of questions that the participating team members found useful but rather the learning spaces that the project provided (e.g., discussions in the capacity-building workshops and working together on the evaluation). Going forward, perhaps the question should not be about what is the best tool but how such tools can should be integrated into evaluation capacity-building workshops and other structures for interaction.

2. *The need for a clear manual*: As part of this project we developed a manual for the guidelines toward the latter part of the project. It would have facilitated the usage of the guidelines if we had the manual before we had started this project. The guidelines would have been more helpful if we had a manual with more examples ready at the time when the workshops were delivered.

3. *The field of equity evaluation is still evolving*: As part of this project we conducted multiple reviews of evaluations of health equity interventions. One of the lessons we learned was that the field of evaluating health equities is still evolving, with some evaluation approaches predominating over others. For instance, there are many good examples of quasi-experimental approaches to health equity interventions in China but fewer good examples of qualitative approaches to health equities in China. The absence of good examples of evaluation of health equity across a diversity of approaches did impede learning about equities. In hindsight, generating one tool that is relevant to multiple evaluation approaches seems ambitious.

4. *The need to trial the guidelines on local community projects*: The three Chinese projects all focused on high-level national policies. Although these policies had a clear equity focus, they were all projects in large governmental policy settings. The guidelines also need to be tested in many other settings including projects led by community organizations and nongovernmental organization initiatives.

5. *The need to trial the guidelines in multiple organizational and country settings*: While this project was ongoing, key members of the CNHDRC and TECCHI evaluation team were also working in other intervention settings in Canada, Chile, and India on multiple equity projects. One of our learnings working in these other settings was that different country and organizational settings have very different views of how best to address equities and also evaluation needs. We think these guidelines can be more salient to a variety of users if they are further developed and trialed in multiple organizational and country settings.

NEW DIRECTIONS FOR EVALUATION • DOI: 10.1002/ev

Learnings across vastly different contexts need to be incorporated in further development of the guidelines.

6. *The need for a more pragmatic, routine-based appreciation of inequities*: Although our guidelines were informed by a realist evaluation lens that attempted to develop a generative understanding of the mechanisms by which inequities could be addressed, in hindsight this was perhaps too theoretical a frame, given that most of the participants were policymakers and practitioners. Stakeholders struggled with the implications of concepts of equities to their daily roles working as program staff or policy implementers. Going forward, more practical examples are needed of how addressing equities can be incorporated into routine practices of policymakers and practitioners. We think providing more practical advice could lead to greater uptake of such guidelines in policy and programmatic settings.

7. *Formal operationalization of ideas might also help conceptually*: One of our initial points of view was to steer clear of very technical notions of inequities and instead stress a more conceptual view of inequities. One of the most useful workshops that participants appreciated was a technical workshop that described how changes in equities could be operationalized using a range of statistical measures. One of the interesting aspects of the workshops was a number of participating stakeholders seemed to develop a more conceptual understanding of equities after they understood statistical operationalizations of how best to measure equities. The lesson here for us was that different groups of learners can understand concepts of equity through different learning approaches. Put differently, for some groups of individuals, at times understanding of formal operationalization of equities might precede a deeper conceptual understanding.

Conclusion: From a Testing to a Developmental Approach

Although our original goal was to use the three projects to test the guidelines, we realized very soon into the implementation that the guidelines needed considerably greater development (Patton, 2010) than we had originally planned. For example, the initial version of the guidelines was very complex. Based on initial feedback from the teams, the initial guidelines were considerably simplified. Given the state of the field of equity evaluation, we determined that a developmental approach to developing and trialing guidelines across settings was needed. We were far too fixated at the early stage of the project on "testing" the guidelines; over time we recognized what was needed was a developmental process (Patton, 2010) to enhance thinking about equities. Additionally, although our approach to guideline development stressed a realist and utilization perspective, we did not sufficiently consider other relevant lenses to health equity including incorporating an explicit social justice focus on equities. In the field of health equity research, there is an increased focus on issues of rights and social justice. We think future versions of guidelines need to more explicitly consider such perspectives at the development stage itself.

References

Commission on Social Determinants of Health. (2008). *Closing the gap in a generation: Health equity through action on the social determinants of health.* Geneva: World Health Organization.
Gardner, B. (2008). Toronto Central LHIN health equity discussion paper. Toronto, ON: Toronto Central Local Health Integration Network.
Graham, H. (2004). Tackling inequalities in health in England: Remedying health disadvantages, narrowing health gaps or reducing health gradients? *Journal of Social Policy, 33*(1), 115–131.
Johnston, L. G., & Sabin, K. (2010). Sampling hard-to-reach populations with respondent driven sampling. *Methodological Innovations Online, 5*(2), 38–48.
Liang, X., Guo, H., Jin, C., Peng, X., & Zhang, X. (2012). The effect of New Cooperative Medical Scheme on health outcomes and alleviating catastrophic health expenditure in China: A systematic review. *PLoS ONE, 7*(8).
Mark, M. M., & Henry, G. T. (2004). The mechanisms and outcomes of evaluation influence. *Evaluation, 10*(1), 35–57. https://doi.org/10.1177/1356389004042326
Patton, M. Q. (2008). *Utilization focused evaluation* (4th ed.). Thousand Oaks, CA: Sage Publications.
Patton, M. Q. (2010). *Developmental evaluation: Applying complexity concepts to enhance innovation and use.* New York, NY: Guilford Press.
Pawson, R. D. (2013). *The science of evaluation: A realist manifesto.* Thousand Oaks, CA: Sage Publications.
Solar, O., & Irwin, A. (2010). *A conceptual framework for action on the social determinants of health* (Social Determinants of Health Discussion Paper 2, Policy and Practice). Geneva: World Health Organization.
Tannahill, C., & Sridharan, S. (2013). Getting real about policy and practice needs: Evaluation as a bridge between the problem and solution space. *Evaluation and Program Planning, 36*(1), 157–164
World Health Organization. (2016a). Equity. Retrieved from http://www.who.int/gender-equity-rights/understanding/equity-definition/en/
World Health Organization. (2016b). Social determinants of health. Retrieved from http://www.who.int/social_determinants/en/

SANJEEV SRIDHARAN is the director of The Evaluation Centre for Complex Health Interventions at St. Michael's Hospital and an associate professor with the Institute of Health Policy, Management and Evaluation at the University of Toronto in Canada.

KUN ZHAO is a professor at the China National Health Development Research Center in Beijing, China.

NEW DIRECTIONS FOR EVALUATION • DOI: 10.1002/ev

APRIL NAKAIMA *is a senior evaluator at The Evaluation Centre for Complex Health Interventions at St. Michael's Hospital in Canada.*

JOANNA MAPLAZI *is a public health professional working in the areas of public health policy, health evaluation, and global health in Toronto, Ontario.*

MO YU *is a research coordinator at The Evaluation Centre for Complex Health Interventions at St. Michael's Hospital in Canada.*

YINGPENG QIU *is a researcher based the China National Health Development Research Center in Beijing, China.*

NEW DIRECTIONS FOR EVALUATION • DOI: 10.1002/ev

Hay, K. (2017). Equity is not an intervention: Implications of evaluation—reflections from india. In S. Sridharan, K. Zhao, & A. Nakaima (Eds.), *Building Capacities to Evaluate Health Inequities: Some Lessons Learned from Evaluation Experiments in China, India and Chile. New Directions for Evaluation, 154,* 79–89.

6

Equity Is Not an Intervention: Implications of Evaluation—Reflections from India

Katherine Hay

Abstract

Like most of the world, China, India, and Chile—the three countries discussed in this volume—are all characterized by increasing inequity. Equity is not the primary goal driving core policies and programs, and equity is often knowingly and readily sacrificed for other goals. In such a context, is it reasonable to expect that interventions generated from systems that perpetuate and deepen inequities, and do not challenge those systems and outcomes, will lead to equity? Is it reasonable to expect further that evaluation of such interventions will enhance equity? This chapter suggests that it is reasonable, but only if such evaluations are understood and framed as intentional disruptions to systems perpetuating inequities. Taking India as an example, the chapter lays out the persistence of health inequities in India and discusses implications and possible solutions emerging from seeing program and other evaluations as an opportunity to disrupt program, organizational, or system ecologies that perpetuate inequities. The chapter sees no conflict between, and argues for, models of evaluation that are both rigorous and transformative. © 2017 Wiley Periodicals, Inc., and the American Evaluation Association.

I n societies where equity is the driving goal, and where collectively citizens, the state, and the media privilege and actively work toward realizing equity, perhaps fairly straightforward evaluations of interventions could increase equity. In such societies evaluation with robust measures and tools could identify the "best" programs, where "best" is defined as reducing inequities. Armed with that knowledge other technocrats would design more of the "right programs" and equity would be achieved.

But these are not our societies.

We live in societies characterized by models of development that perpetuate and reinforce inequity and/or consider equity a luxury to be sought after more basic needs are met. Like most of the world, China, India, and Chile—the three countries discussed in this volume—are all characterized by increasing inequity. Equity is not the primary goal driving core policies and programs, and equity is often knowingly and readily sacrificed for other goals.

So how can evaluation increase equity here? Is it reasonable to expect that interventions generated from systems that perpetuate and deepen inequities will lead to equity? Is it reasonable to expect that evaluation of such interventions will enhance equity?

The chapter suggests it is reasonable, and indeed a needed aspiration, but is possible only if evaluations are understood and framed as intentional disruptions to inequitable systems. Equity will not be reached through an intervention or even a set of interventions; rather, building equitable societies entails taking a stance that we value equity. Doing so necessitates bringing this lens to all that we do, including evaluation. In such a view, equity will not be achieved with technical tinkering on the sidelines of existing systems that perpetuate inequities. Equity will entail rethinking what matters. We see this rethinking in movements, mass protest, elections, and public discourse. Seeing evaluation as part of that change, entails seeing evaluation as having the potential to both (a) leave inequities and inequitable systems unchallenged (thus holding up the status quo) or (b) use evaluation, as with other work and tools, to challenge the status quo and hold a mirror to it. After laying out the evidence on the persistence of health inequities in India, this chapter discusses implications and possible solutions emerging from the second evaluation stance.

The Persistence of Inequities, with the Example of India

The intent of this chapter is not to lay out new insights on the level and persistence of inequities in India. Examples of economic and health inequities are flagged to lay the context for the remainder of the chapter.

Despite robust growth, the Gini coefficient for India (the most frequently recognized measurement of economic inequity) shows an increasing trend since the 1990s in income inequality (from 30.8% to 33.9%) laid over existing large variation in poverty rates among social groups (by tribe, caste, and religion) in India and across states (Panagariya, 2014). If we turn to health, whereas on average, health outcomes have improved, the gains are not even. Caste, gender, class, religion, and region remain systemic, institutional, and social determinants of outcomes that influence everything from anemia to immunizations (Balarajan, Fawzi, & Subramanian, 2013). There are wide differences across states, reflected in vastly different mortality rates and life expectancies for different populations.

To give just a few examples:

- Female life expectancy is 67 in Uttar Pradesh versus 78 in Kerala (Ministry of Health and Family Welfare [MoHFW], 2011).
- A woman in Uttar Pradesh is almost five times more likely to die during childbirth than a woman in Kerala (Registrar General & Census Commissioner, 2013).
- A child in Bihar is twice as likely to die before turning 5, compared to a child in Tamil Nadu (International Institute for Population Sciences [IIPS] & Macro International, 2007a).
- A child from the lowest wealth quintile in Bihar is 10 times more likely to be severely underweight, compared to a child from the highest wealth quintile (IIPS & Macro International, 2007b).
- A child from a scheduled caste (a historically marginalized group) is twice as likely to be severely stunted and underweight as a child who is not (Ministry of Women and Child Development [MWCD], 2014).

Disparities by geography, income, and caste are compounded by gender inequities. For example, Table 6.1 shows some gender gaps in one of the largest and poorest states in India, Uttar Pradesh (UP). The sex ratio at

Table 6.1. Gender Gaps in Girls' and Boys' Health in UP

Girls have differential and poorer health outcomes compared to boys in UP

	Girls	Boys
Infant mortality rate (per 1,000 live births)*	71	69
Under-5 mortality rate (per 1,000 live births)*	97	88
Underweight[†]	43.7%	41.2%

Attention to health is worse for 0- to 5-year-old girls than boys in UP

After controlling for socioeconomic and demographic characteristics, girls are 1.36 times more likely not to receive any treatment for "any morbidity" compared to boys[†]

Mothers are 43% less likely to report female newborn illness compared to male newborns[‡]

Average expenditure on male newborns is four times higher than on female newborns[‡]

65% of male neonates are taken to private practitioners compared to 43% of female neonates[‡]

*Annual Health Survey 2011–2012
[†]National Family Health Survey (NFHS) round 3, 2005–06
[‡]Willis J. R. et al. Gender differences in perception and care-seeking for illness of newborns in rural Uttar Pradesh, India, *Journal of Health, Population and Nutrition*, 27(1), 62–71

birth (911) in UP was higher than the overall child sex ratio (899) implying postnatal neglect of the girl child in her infant years (0–6).

What Does Any of This Have to Do with Evaluation?

As the examples presented here suggest, development is not an inevitable march toward equity. Development pathways shape and determine the nature of programs and particularly the extent to which equity is prioritized or not prioritized. Despite, for example, strong economic growth in India, we have seen growth without growing equity in several areas. If evaluation does not illustrate those inequities, it can reinforce them. For example, looking only at average improvements can obscure growing inequities. Going further, even studies that highlight inequities do not always analyze or critique the system dynamics that underlie the problem of inequities. Inequities are thus, taken as given—as a necessary if unfortunate externality of development; in this way the social construct of the inevitability of inequity is reinforced.

Ignoring the larger socioeconomic system and development models obscures or ignores their inherent valuation of some outcomes over others. The hazard of seeing evaluation as external to those systems is to ignore the biases in dominant pathways or the way some things are valued over others. Those same biases and values are then implicitly replicated in evaluations.

An implication of doing evaluation within systems that either reinforce, create, perpetuate, or ignore inequities is the need to see those systems and to see evaluation as part of those systems. However, this broadened view also offers the possibility to see evaluation as a potential disruption in those systems.

Ignoring the disruptive potential of evaluation, or the possibility that the evaluation and evaluation process can encompass other values, is to reduce evaluation to a technocratic exercise of propping up the status quo—including both unjust systems of development and unjust programs operating within them. To do all of this under the cloak of "science" and "rigor" is to inherently reduce both of these ideas and to strip them of their deeper meanings.

From Observer to Disruptor

To be meaningful and relevant to addressing persistent and deepening inequities, evaluation needs a fundamental reorientation from being an external observer of the system to being an internal disrupter of the system. Historically, evaluation has drawn heavily from technocratic traditions and distance. Perhaps nowhere is this truer than evaluations in public health. Indeed, in both public health and evaluation, the moorings of disinterest or detachment are often used to claim greater rigor or ability to judge merit or worth.

New Directions for Evaluation • DOI: 10.1002/ev

Detached evaluation is both an illusion and a very limiting stance in addressing health inequities. Evaluation does not operate outside of systems. Systems shape what gets evaluated, which questions get asked, and which do not. Confusing rigor with detachment, and understanding detachment to mean taking any questions of value presented by the evaluation commissioner as the only questions of value, provides little scope for engaging on equity within a pathway that prioritizes changes in aggregate over changes on the margins.

Davidson (2014) elegantly argues: "Evaluative reasoning is an inherently value-infused task ... Getting the 'values' part right is the core of evaluation's validity" (p. 32). Doing that, she argues, entails asking: "Does the evidence gathered adequately capture the realities for those who have historically been marginalized or underserved by the system?" and has the evaluation "become a positive force for change by delivering value-infused ... insights [to underpin] ... action for social betterment (Henry, 2000)" (p. 32).

If the fundamental purpose of evaluation is valuing—part of the role of the evaluator is to ask questions of "whose values?" and "what is being valued?" and to transparently bring more inclusive values, including equity, into those discussions using whatever tools and openings are appropriate.

These are not new arguments. Branches of evaluation rooted in epistemologies of participation do provide alternative understandings of rigor that come from engagement; most apply that lens to understand interventions within inequitable systems, some attempt to resist those systems. Transformative evaluators argue that evaluation needs to be conducted within a framework whose goals are to increase social justice for disenfranchised groups (Mertens, 2009, p. 4). Feminist evaluators also frame evaluation as being itself both a product of existing systems and a complex intervention and layer political understandings, including of resistance and engagement, onto such frameworks (Hay, 2014a). Transformative participatory evaluation is intentionally disruptive and argues for the inclusion of the poor in the interpretation of the impact of development efforts (Cousins & Whitmore, 1998). The rest of this chapter connects the idea of equity-oriented evaluation to health inequities and frames evaluations as intentional disruptions to health systems (including program, organization, development, and social systems). What does being disruptive and taking a stance actually look like? The following example demonstrates how such frameworks, combined with intentionality and accountability for equity, can generate ecologies of evidence (see Editors' Notes in this volume) that help push systems toward greater equity.

An Equity-Oriented Evaluation Story from India

In Bihar, India, since 2012, the Bill and Melinda Gates Foundation has partnered with the state government on ambitious maternal and child health goals. At the beginning of 2012, baseline data from over 13,000 women who had delivered the previous year was collected across the state. We had data on gender, birth parity, caste, income, religion, etc. But having disaggregated data does not mean we had gender and equity covered. The baseline report (Rangarajan et al., 2013) had some subgroup analysis but gender and equity had not been a core focus. Although the program team, when asked, certainly hoped to reduce inequities, the data were not being fully optimized to pursue this goal nor was reduction in inequity a core program focus.

On aggregate, the baseline data showed gaps in maternal services and coverage for all women. In asking "whose experiences are not reflected?" further analysis revealed large differences among women. For example, using the same baseline data, Figure 6.1 shows the differences between women who were more or less advantaged (by caste/religious group, wealth quartiles, and literacy).

Although from the baseline we knew that most women (72%) on average were not getting adequate antenatal care (ANC), equity analysis showed large variations among women. Only 16% of the most marginalized women were receiving at least three or more antenatal checkups compared to 54% of the less marginalized. As I captured in a blog at the time:

> At this point the midline was upon us. We were only weeks away from being able to examine whether inequities had been reduced two years on.
>
> With more detailed analysis of inequities in hand, we asked the team whether they expected the program to reduce inequities, hold them constant, or widen them. This created a surge of interest in results for marginalized groups at midline. Evaluation can lead as well as follow.
>
> In hindsight the choice to deepen this analysis and use it to engage with programs sounds like just doing good evaluation. And it is. But the point is that it doesn't just happen. We make choices about what to look at all the time. (Hay, 2014b, para. 9–11)

Knowing that equity gaps were being analyzed brought a focus at midline on whether the program would reduce inequities, hold them constant, or widen them.

At midline, outcomes for marginalized women had indeed improved in a number of areas. The program had substantially improved outcomes for marginalized women in several areas including frontline worker visits, breastfeeding, complementary feeding, and use of modern methods of family planning (Borkum et al., 2014). Although large gaps between more and less marginalized women remained, the focus on inequities encouraged the program teams to focus on inequities. They are now identifying evidence-based mechanisms and strategies to further drive reductions in inequities.

NEW DIRECTIONS FOR EVALUATION • DOI: 10.1002/ev

Figure 6.1. Inequalities at Baseline Among Women in Bihar Who Delivered a Child the Previous Year

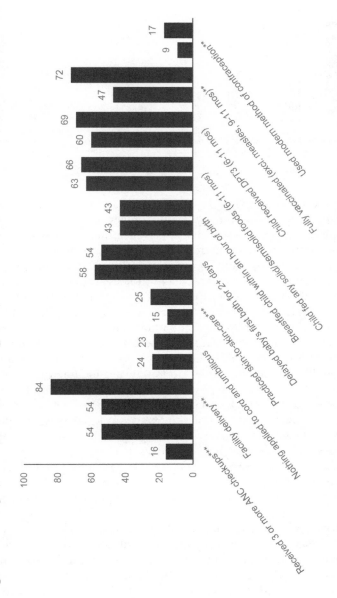

■ SC/ST or Muslim, Wealth Quartile 1, Illiterate   ■ Non-SC/ST, Non-Muslim, Wealth Quartile 4, Literate

Note: Estimates regression adjust for woman's age, parity, district, and rural location: $p < 0.10$, $p < 0.05$, $p < 0.01$ for regression-adjusted difference.

Figure 6.2. Abuse and Controlling Behavior Reported by Women in Bihar

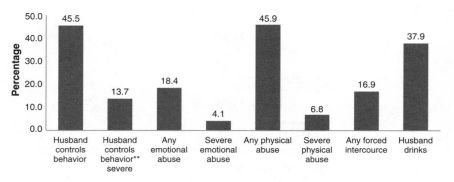

Note: N = 11,151

Building on these efforts, the Gates Foundation's India office built a gender equity lens into the country health strategy and is establishing metrics around equity to ensure that this lens is meaningful. In valuing equity, the evaluation process promoted the generation and use of data in ways that generated new knowledge and new conversations around inequity. That process made inequities explicit and made choices around the value placed on closing those inequities also explicit. The choice made was to make gender and other equities an explicit and measured value going forward.

As discussed earlier in the chapter, understanding evaluation as a disruptive element situated within larger socioeconomic and development systems entails also understanding how those systems reinforce inequities. Even studies that include inequities do not always include the system dynamics that underlie inequities. With this in view, the evaluation team also added questions to the midline on intimate partner violence, husband control, and other potential drivers of gender inequities—areas the program was not explicitly working on.

Unsurprisingly, early analysis found high levels of violence against women (see Figure 6.2). Forty-five percent of the women surveyed reported having experienced physical abuse, among which 16% had experienced forced sexual intercourse. The prevalence of abuse was higher among more marginalized women.

We also looked at the relationship of this violence to key maternal and child health behaviors. Women facing physical abuse were less likely to deliver at facilities and carry out exclusive breastfeeding for their infants (Borkum et al., 2014). Preliminary analysis shows higher intimate partner violence is associated with higher likelihood of miscarriage, stillbirths, and pregnancy complications.

This inclusion of abuse and controlling behavior in an evaluation of a program not working on either reflects attention to the larger systems in which programs operate. Examining inequities is meaningless without understanding the institutions, relations, and norms that underpin and perpetuate them. Seeing evaluations as operating within larger systems, entails building out ecologies of evidence that may also go beyond the specific evaluation questions being addressed. Evidence cannot take us in new directions (and challenge the status quo) if we limit evidence collection to what we are already doing.

Including these components in the evaluation was not to make a judgment about what worked to reduce violence or controlling behaviors but to generate new knowledge about factors shaping and perpetuating inequities. That knowledge might, in turn, lead to more informed decision making should the evaluation stakeholders be compelled, through the evaluation, to bring more attention to inequities.

The idea here is that paying attention to inequities can entail expanding the lens beyond the program (for causes and solutions) and, for example, building out health and nonhealth interventions that might disrupt inequities. A key point here is that moving from a detached observer role to an active disruptor has very distinct implications on how one understands the role of specific evaluations. A disruptor who sees evaluation as part of a larger evidence ecosystem (as opposed to a contained, stand-alone, confined output) will see that evaluation as part of evolving bodies of work, organizations, fields of understanding, and, yes, development pathways. A disruptor will not believe that equity will be reached through an intervention, or even a set of interventions, that are "over there," but rather sees the task of building equitable societies as a shared responsibility, "starting here." Doing so entails bringing an equity lens to all that we do, including evaluation. That framing makes it natural to be thinking, "what will come next" in the journey of our organizations and areas of work, "what questions will we then be asking?" This prompts us to anticipate, preempt, and create the conditions for those questions, and in so doing, amplify the ability of any particular evaluation to move that conversation further.

Although this may seem relatively easy to do, anyone who has designed an evaluation knows that real trade-offs are involved. Space and time are limited and asking some questions means not asking others or the costs of the work and people's time can increase. It can be easier to say, "not within the scope—not my job" than to argue to include equity. The power hierarchies in evaluation can make this particularly difficult for consultants attempting to convince funders. Either way, whether the evaluation is driven by the evaluation commissioner or evaluator, there is an opportunity cost to including new areas of knowledge, particularly when we are not directly working on them. There can also be political barriers to including a focus on equity when and if commissioners fear negative findings. But disrupting inequities entails making space in knowledge creation to insert them in.

In the example described, without compromising on rigor, adding equity analysis and questions on social norms allowed us to capture insights on health outcomes (the goal of the program) but also on equity. Given that paths to equity are not simply technical—having data on the relationships between inequities and how gender and social norms influence health outcomes enabled us to use our evaluation to influence the conversation on our health work.

The results of this evaluative process were ready at a time when the foundation was more intentionally looking at gender (Gates, 2014). In this case, the intent to disrupt landed in a space ready to be disrupted. The creation of this evidence leads to new investments on equity and violence and to new goals around gender and equity. It does not always work like this. If it did inequities would not be so persistent. The point is that just as the foundation will change through that intentionality, that disruption, so too evaluation also has to become more intentional about disrupting inequities. Evaluators need to take that on.

Although the results came at an opportune time, the point from an equity informed disruptive stance is not to wait for a policy or dialogue window to open. I did not wait for someone to instruct me to ask those questions. I included them because I believed if I had evidence on the factors and inequities underpinning health, the evaluation process could open that window, creative positive disruption, and my colleagues and partners working to improve women's health would act. Just as the foundation has to be accountable for their intentionality around closing equity gaps—so too do we as evaluators also have that responsibility.

Working to bring an equity lens into our evaluation practice does not weaken the rigor of evaluation; it makes explicit whether equity is valued or not, and, in raising these questions we make our own values transparent. The field of evaluation is not composed of observers; evaluators are participants in the way development unfolds. Evaluators need to take a position on equity, be transparent on the value we place on it and be active in measuring it with the tools and techniques at our disposal. If we do not, we are simply reinforcing existing biases within development pathways by not making transparent and explicit the values that are being ignored.

References

Balarajan, Y. S., Fawzi, W. W., & Subramanian, S. V. (2013). Changing patterns of social inequalities in anaemia among women in India: Cross-sectional study using nationally representative data. BMJ Open, 3(3). https://doi.org/10.1136/bmjopen-2012-002233

Borkum, E., Rangarajan, A., Shridharan, S., Rotz, D., Manoranjini, M., Morgan, S., ... Singh, P. (2014). Midline findings from the evaluation of Ananya Program in Bihar. Princeton, NJ: Mathematica Policy Research.

Cousins, J. B., & Whitmore, E. (1998), Framing participatory evaluation. New Directions for Evaluation, 1998: 5–23. https://doi.org/10.1002/ev.1114

Davidson, E. J. (2014). How "beauty" can bring truth and justice to life. In J. C. Griffith & B. Montrosse-Moorhead (Eds.), New Directions for Evaluation: No. 142. Revisiting truth, beauty, and justice: Evaluating with validity in the 21st century (pp. 31–43). San Francisco, CA: Jossey-Bass.

Gates, M. (2014). Putting women and girls at the center of development. *Science, 345*, 1273–1275. https://doi.org/10.1126/science.1258882

Hay, K. (2014a). Feminist evaluation in South Asia: Building bridges of theory and practice. In S. Brisolara, D. Seigart, & S. SenGupta (Eds.), *Feminist evaluation and research: Theory and practice* (pp. 197–223). New York, NY: Guilford Press.

Hay, K. (2014b, November 4). Letting the evidence lead: Good evaluation means taking a position on equity [Web log post]. Retrieved from https://ieg.worldbankgroup.org/blog/letting-evidence-lead-good-evaluation-means-taking-position-equity

International Institute for Population Sciences & Macro International. (2007b). *National Family Health Survey (NFHS-4), 2015–16: India: Vol. II*. Mumbai, India: Author.

International Institute for Population Sciences & Macro International. (2007a). *National Family Health Survey (NFHS-3), 2005–06: India: Vol. II*. Mumbai, India: Author.

Mertens, D. M. (2009). *Transformative research and evaluation*. New York, NY: Guilford Press.

Ministry of Health and Family Welfare. (2011). *Family welfare statistics in India*. New Delhi, India: Author.

Ministry of Women and Child Development. (2014). *Rapid Survey on Children (RSOC) 2013–14*. New Delhi, India: Author.

Panagariya, A., & More, V. (2014). Poverty by social, religious and economic groups in India and its largest states: 1993–1994 to 2011–2012. *Indian Growth and Development Review, 7*(2), 202–230. https://doi.org/10.1108/IGDR-03-2014-0007

Rangarajan, A., Borkum, E., Sridharan, S., Rotz, D., Manoranjini, M., Morgan, S., ... Kumar, G. A. (2013). *Baseline findings from the Ananya Evaluation*. Princeton, NJ: Mathematica Policy Research.

Registrar General, & Census Commissioner, India. (2013). *SRS statistical reports 2013*.

KATHERINE HAY *is a gender and development expert, currently leading both the evaluation and gender equality programming of the Bill and Melinda Gates Foundation in India.*

NEW DIRECTIONS FOR EVALUATION • DOI: 10.1002/ev

Das, A. (2017). The challenge of evaluating equity in health: Experiences from India's maternal health program. In S. Sridharan, K. Zhao, & A. Nakaima (Eds.), *Building Capacities to Evaluate Health Inequities: Some Lessons Learned from Evaluation Experiments in China, India and Chile. New Directions for Evaluation*, 154, 91–100.

7

The Challenge of Evaluating Equity in Health: Experiences from India's Maternal Health Program

Abhijit Das

Abstract

This paper raises questions about the impacts of one of India's most ambitious cash conditional transfer programs, Janani Suraksha Yojana. It incorporates the perspectives of a practitioner working on maternal health issues and discusses the importance of considering alternative explanations as part of any patterns of observed results. It argues for exploring the impacts of interventions on the most vulnerable and marginalized as an essential aspect of an equity evaluation and for exploring impacts on inequities from a human rights lens. It also discusses some of the core competencies that might be needed for evaluations of equity initiatives. © 2017 Wiley Periodicals, Inc., and the American Evaluation Association.

My interest in evaluation began years ago when as a young physician I was unable to reconcile what I saw of people's lives and their health in the remote villages in India where I worked and what I read about the implementation of a national health program in that same province. The reported "achievements" of the health program didn't match with my experience of the dysfunctional health system on the ground. Now having spent over a decade as a rural physician and twice as many years as a health systems researcher and human rights advocate engaging with the public health system in the interest of marginalized communities, I see this gap as the challenge of understanding and addressing inequity. Health inequity as we now agree relates to the avoidable and the unfair differences in health status among different groups. Thus, one not only needs to identify the differences in health determinants and outcomes but also make judgments about fairness and acceptability.

Today equity has been center-staged as an independent Sustainable Development Goal by the United Nations. Goal 10 calls for reducing inequality within and among countries. In order to support the achievement of this goal the role of evaluation is crucial, not only to identify inequality but also to engage with the process of design and implementation by contributing to developing pertinent program theories and monitoring progress through appropriate indicators. But in order to fulfill these responsibilities, the evaluation practitioner must be familiar with the limitations inherent in current practice. In this paper, I identify some of the pitfalls in the way evaluation is practiced currently using the example of India's Janani Suraksha Yojana (JSY or Maternal Protection Scheme), a conditional cash transfer program introduced in 2005 to reduce maternal mortality. Since JSY was introduced maternal death rates have reduced considerably. But as a health systems researcher I have visited different provinces of the country where life-saving interventions like cesarean section or blood transfusion are unavailable and women continue to die in unacceptably large numbers. For me this raises an interesting evaluation conundrum. How can the evaluator support the program manager with appropriate analyses to reconcile the two contradicting realities to make better decisions? Is the decline in maternal mortality sufficient evidence for the success of the intervention (JSY) even in the absence of adequate life-saving facilities? Are there any alternate explanations? What are the consequences of making a mistaken judgment, especially for the lives of marginalized people? Using my own experience, research findings, and program evaluation data I try not only to answer these questions but also to identify some of the core competencies that evaluators need to develop if they are to contribute effectively to the new development paradigm where the values of equity, inclusion, and human rights are increasingly being seen as paramount.

An Introduction to NRHM and JSY

A new national government was elected in India in May 2004 and it launched the National Rural Health Mission (NRHM) in April 2005 with the goal of improving the "availability of and access to quality health care by people, especially for those residing in rural areas, the poor, women and children" (Ministry of Health and Family Welfare [MoHFW], 2005, p. 1). This was also the same time when global interest in the reduction of childhood and maternal mortality was rising because of the Millennium Development Goals 4 and 5 (MDG) review process. According to data available at that time the maternal mortality rate (MMR) in India was considered to be

NEW DIRECTIONS FOR EVALUATION • DOI: 10.1002/ev

very high, amounting to nearly one fourth of the 500,000 maternal deaths globally. The NRHM goal was to reduce MMR to 100 for every 100,000 live births by 2012. In order to achieve this goal India adapted the internationally recommended approach of focusing on intrapartum care (Campbell et al., 2006) by prescribing institutional childbirth for all deliveries, promoted by the conditional cash transfer scheme JSY in 2005. Between 2005–2006 and 2013–2014 the number of women receiving JSY benefits increased from 730,000 to over 10.5 million (MoHFW, 2014) and over 104.5 billion rupees had been paid as incentives over these 9 years (Press Information Bureau, 2013).

Reconciling Contradictory Evidence—An Evaluation Challenges

When the NRHM was launched in 2005 there was a concern in India that MMR was not declining and the first two rounds of the National Family Health Survey (NFHS) in 1992–1993 and 1998–1999 had shown an increase from 424 to 540 (Registrar General of India [RGI], 2006). However, soon after the NRHM was launched the results of a much more rigorous survey showed that the all-India MMR of 398 in 1997–1998 had actually come down to 301 in 2001–2003 (RGI, 2006). Subsequent estimates of maternal mortality through the same methodology continued to show an overall decline in MMR to 254 in 2004–2006 to 212 in 2007–2009 and then to 167 in 2011–2013. At the same time estimates of institutional delivery, which were a low 41% in 2005–2006 (NFHS 3) when NRHM started, have risen steadily and were estimated to be 78.7% in 2013–2014 (Ministry of Women and Child Development, 2015). These two indicators in terms of inputs and results appeared to bear testimony to the success of JSY and associated intervention and its implied assumptions.

Although the overall results were moving in the desired and anticipated directions, other information was unsettling. The decline in maternal mortality was far less in poor rural populations and access to services in these areas continued to be poor (Montgomery et al., 2015). The data emerging from the Annual Health Surveys (AHS) showed that the proportion of maternal deaths in the 25 worst-off divisions (an administrative division bigger than a district but smaller than a province) had risen from 41% to 45% across three rounds of the AHS. Also 207 out of 284 high-focus districts remained in the same range of MMR across the first two rounds. Similarly, 67 districts had shown an increase or no decline in neonatal mortality in the same period. A large-scale review (Lim et al., 2010) concluded that JSY had indeed increased rates of institutional delivery but, although there was a slight reduction in perinatal and neonatal death, there was no effect on maternal death. This study also noted that the intended targeting of the most vulnerable was not happening. It was also pointed out that the increase in institutional delivery attributed to JSY could be a fallacy (Das, Rao, & Hagopian, 2011).

Subsequent reviews of JSY have uniformly been less enthusiastic about its impact on quality of care of basic delivery services, referral services for emergencies (Chaturvedi, Randive, Diwan, & De Costa, 2014), and ability to provide better services for marginalized populations like those living in slums (Vikram, Sharma, & Kannan, 2013), minority communities (Nasir, 2014), hard-to-reach populations, and so on (Khan, Hazra, & Bhatnagar, 2010). The availability of life-saving services like blood transfusion or emergency cesarean section had not been provided in all high-focus districts. On the other hand, the cost of delivery services remains high (Modugu, Kumar, & Millet, 2012). Thus although JSY has been able to bring many more women to have institutional delivery, the quality of delivery, referral, and emergency obstetric services has not improved as anticipated. Also JSY has not been able to address issues of equity and mortality rates have shown the least decline in those districts and states where it was high to start with. A nine-state review of 5 years' data on JSY has found no association in increase of institutional delivery with reduction in maternal mortality, and the inequality of access to services continues despite JSY (Ranadive, San Sebastian, De Costa, & Lindholm, 2014).

Interpreting the Findings to Make a Programmatic Judgment

In order to make informed judgments from the information at hand the evaluator needs to understand the nature of the evidence, the program theory and associated assumptions, the population characteristics of the intended beneficiaries, and their interaction with the program as well as alternate pathways, explanations, and possibilities.

Understanding the Nature of the Evidence

Before NRHM India followed the broad outlines of the Demographic and Health Surveys (DHS) in its NFHS but in 2008 the Ministry of Health conducted the modified District Level Household Survey (DLHS) to obtain district-level data that were earlier not available through the NFHS. However, immediately afterwards another modified district-level survey called AHS was started for the 284 high-focus districts of NRHM. The AHS however was not powered to provide social group or caste disaggregated data. Thus as the NRHM rolled out there was no information on social parameters like caste, tribe, or religion that are known to affect service access and outcomes and contribute to inequity. In the absence of these crucial variables it is difficult to do sophisticated modeling exercises, but some have been attempted and those too do not yield any positive results for JSY.

Some specific studies were also conducted to understand the implementation of the JSY and these indicated that although the financial incentive was indeed drawing poor women to institutional delivery, the quality of care of basic as well as emergency obstetric services were poor

(National Health Systems Resource Centre [NHRSC], 2011; United Nations Population Fund, 2009). Independent studies into the lack of effectiveness and gaps of JSY have already been reported earlier. A ministry-sponsored evaluation of the JSY (NHSRC, 2011) concluded that there was a need to strengthen the different provisions of an institutional delivery-based system, which was not working optimally, without for once considering an alternative approach. The overall assumption here appeared to be that the package of JSY and institutional delivery for all women was the "only" solution and all measures that could enable this solution were the only appropriate next steps.

Understanding Social Marginalization and Multiple Social Realities

Data from earlier NFHS indicated that communities from excluded social groups like scheduled castes and tribes have significantly poorer maternal health indicators as well as lower access to services. A large proportion of the population in India is socially marginalized with 17% being from Scheduled Castes, 9% are Tribal, and 14 % are from the Muslim minority community. A large number of people live in extremely remote locations. 82 out of 604 districts in the country officially considered to have Left Wing Extremism (LWE). According to the third round of AHS 42 districts (out of 284) continued to be "hotspots" because they showed low coverage for antenatal care, institutional delivery, and immunization. These data indicate that a large proportion of the population could be deprived from the benefits of good quality services either due to remoteness or social exclusion. An equity perspective in evaluation demands that the evaluator be aware of this dimension. Thus to bring women to a system that cannot promise benefits and potentially causes harm violates the basic ethical principle of "do no harm."

Unfortunately as has been pointed out earlier, the currently available datasets do not provide caste-based disaggregation so one has to look for other sources of information. A series of case studies about tribal women who died during pregnancy, childbirth, or the postnatal period in Godda, a tribal district in Jharkhand (John, Singh, & Bannerjee, 2013) shows that the women either did not receive the anticipated services or when they called for these services in times of emergency, these were not made available. A study conducted by me and colleagues (Contractor & Das, 2015) among tribal communities in Kalyanpur block of Raygada district of Orissa showed that the health system was completely ignorant about the traditional pregnancy, delivery, and childcare practices of these tribal communities. Without any understanding of the lived realities of tribal communities the frontline health workers, who belonged to a different community, were trying to get these women to follow the prescribed regimen without much success. The community had certain rituals to ensure the health of mother and infant and they visited a set of providers who in certain situations did

NEW DIRECTIONS FOR EVALUATION • DOI: 10.1002/ev

refer them to modern medical facilities. Anthropologists (Jeffery, Jeffery, & Lyon, 1989; Pinto, 2006) have earlier indicated the diverse range of cultural practices associated with pregnancy, childbirth, and infant care across the country. However, the public health system has made little effort to understand or incorporate existing practices and situate the new prescribed practices within the existing community concerns.

In addition to systemic oversight one also needs to be conversant with the potential for more deliberate human rights violations that are possible in such a hierarchical situation. In conversation with service providers in many districts I have found that that such marginalized communities were further stigmatized and castigated for not appreciating the various arrangements that had been made, or not contributing to the "national cause." This can be considered adding insult to injury or double jeopardy because in some cases the women did not come to institutional delivery because they did not perceive the services as being good and had heard of or faced adverse experiences or harassment.

Questioning the Solution: Understanding the Program Theory and Assumptions

The concurrent increase in institutional delivery and reduction of maternal mortality leads to a simplistic assumption that increased institutional delivery must be responsible for this improvement. However, the first in-depth examination into maternal mortality (RGI, 2006) showed that the reduction in maternal mortality had begun before JSY had been started, so the decline that continued was probably nothing more than a secular trend. Also the relationship between reduction in maternal mortality and institutional delivery is based on the assumption that home-based delivery is potentially unsafe for all women, and when such women have delivery in institutions they will get good-quality services, appropriate referral, and high-quality life-saving services when needed. Unfortunately, all these three conditions—high-quality delivery services, referral services, and life-saving emergency obstetric care services—are still not universally available in all districts, raising questions about the internal validity of the results and its relationship with the intervention. On the other hand in some of the high-focus states and districts the institutional delivery rate continued to be below 60% (AHS, 2012–13), thus over 40% women in these places were now no longer able to access home-based support that they could have got earlier from a trained traditional birth attendant (TBA) who was trained to support home-based delivery and identify and refer emergencies. TBA training was soon discontinued after the launch of NRHM in order to discourage home deliveries. So the current reality indicates that many women are not assured safety when they come to institutions and then again many women continue to be exposed to potentially life-threatening situations of home delivery, raising questions around the ethical soundness of the solution.

In Search of Alternatives

The reduction of maternal death with the concurrent increase in institutional delivery would indicate an immediate vindication of the original assumption. However, a good evaluator needs to double check and an old principle called Occam's Razor is an interesting tool to apply to test the plausibility of the explanation. According to this principle, the explanation with the fewest assumptions is probably the preferable one. In the case of JSY and institutional delivery, existing evidence seems to indicate that the basic assumption of getting women to high-quality life-saving services is not met, and thus this is probably not the most effective solution for reducing maternal death for marginalized women or those living in remote locations. A search for alternatives reveals that participatory interventions among tribal communities in Jharkhand in India (Tripathy et al., 2010) have shown definite reductions in maternal and infant mortality. Similar community-based interventions have shown results in Bangladesh (Rowen, Prata, & Passano, 2009), Pakistan (Jokhio, Winter, & Cheng, 2005), and Nepal (Morrison et al., 2010). However, these have not been considered for adaptation for inclusion within the framework of NRHM, suggesting a rigidity of approach and a lack of appreciation of contextual realities.

Discussion

India's maternal health story between 2005 and 2015 took place within a context of increasing global attention to maternal health-related intervention through the monitoring of Millennium Development Goals 4 and 5 related to child health and maternal health and setting up of various international mechanisms like the Maternal Health Task Force (MHTF), the Partnership for Maternal and Newborn and Child Health (PMNCH), and Women Deliver. As the largest contributor to maternal death worldwide, reductions in MMR in India were seen as extremely important. The success of India's JSY was also important because it was based on a variation of the globally recommended solution and any questions here would have an important bearing on the overall approach or theory of change which underpinned this global effort. The reduction of MMR in India was also being held up as an example of possibilities that would be relevant to other places notably in sub-Saharan Africa. And above all there were increasing donor investments in the field of maternal and child health (Dieleman et al., 2016) that were looking for evidence of scalable and replicable interventions.

The evaluator in this case thus is working within a larger sociopolitical context and has probably an even more important role to play. Research skills are important but alone will not be sufficient to negotiate a political minefield. There may be a temptation to play a supportive role to the donors who need "success stories" to justify their investments, or the international program managers who also need those "clues" to show that their programs are proceeding in the right direction. On the high table of development planning and review, the pressure to show evidence to justify past decisions on which currently millions of dollars have been invested could be high. And there may be just enough grey area as shown in the story of JSY. Here the virtue of integrity is crucial for the evaluator. How does the evaluator stitch together the story that emerges from the evidence that has been collected? Do assumptions made in one social context hold true in a different place? Whose interest matters most, and what role do they play in determining the solutions and outcomes? To take the example of a game of football or soccer, what role does the evaluator play? Can the evaluator be the spectator, passionate but powerless to influence the game. Or is the evaluator like the match statistician who keeps a record of all the moves and goals and attempts, records of immense value after the game is over. I believe the evaluator is more like the referee who has responsibility to use observations to blow the whistle and intervene when rules are breached. And to this the evaluator will require a wide range of observational, analytic, and interpretive competencies encompassing the statistical as well as the social and cultural domains to look for alternative evidence and explanations, the courage to question the original program theories and finally the moral integrity to be true to the overall purpose of equity and realization of rights of the most marginalized.

References

Annual Health Survey 2012–2013 Fact Sheet, http://www.censusindia.gov.in/vital_statist ics/AHSBulletins/AHS_Factsheets_2012_13.html (accessed on April 17, 2017)

Campbell, O. M., Graham, W. J., & Lancet Maternal Survival Series Steering Group. (2006). Strategies for reducing maternal mortality: Getting on with what works. *Lancet, 368*, 1284–1299.

Chaturvedi S., Randive, B., Diwan, V., & De Costa, A. (2014). Quality of obstetric referral services in India's JSY cash transfer programme for institutional births: A study from Madhya Pradesh Province. *PLoS One, 9*(5), e96773.

Contractor S., & Das, A. (2015). *Does one-size-fit-all?: Re-evaluating the approach to address Maternal Health of Tribal Communities in India.* Paper presented at the 13th Development Dialogue "The ghosts of MDG: Unpacking the logics of development" at ISS The Hague, November 4–5.

Das A., Rao, D., & Hagopian A. (2011). India's Janani Suraksha Yojana: Further review needed. *Lancet, 377*, 295–296.

Dieleman, J. L., Schneider, M. T., Haakenstad, A., Singh, L., Sadat, N., Birger, M. … Murray, C. J. L. (2016, April 12). Development assistance for health: Past trends, associations, and the future of international financial flows for health. *Lancet.* https://doi.org/10.1016/S0140-6736(16)30168-4

Jeffery, P., Jeffery, R., & Lyon, A. (1989). *Labour pains and labour power: Women and childbearing in India.* London, England: Zed Books.

John, P., Singh, S., & Bannerjee, S. (2013). Stairway to death. *Economic and Political Weekly, 48*(31).

Jokhio, A. H., Winter, H. R., Cheng, K. K. (2005). An intervention involving traditional birth attendants and perinatal and maternal mortality in Pakistan. *New England Journal of Medicine, 352*(20), 2091–2099.

Khan, M. E., Hazra, A., & Bhatnagar, I. (2010). Impact of Janani Suraksha Yojana on selected family health behaviours in rural Uttar Pradesh. *Journal of Family Welfare, 56*, 9–22.

Lim, S. S., Dandona, L., Hoisington, J. A., James, S. L., Hogan, M. C., & Gakidou, E. (2010). India's Janani Suraksha Yojana, a conditional cash transfer programme to increase births in health facilities: An impact evaluation. *Lancet, 375*, 2009–2023.

Ministry of Health and Family Welfare, Government of India. (2005). *NRHM mission document.*

Ministry of Health and Family Welfare, Government of India. (2014). *Annual report 2013–2014.*

Ministry of Women and Child Development, Government of India. (2015). *Rapid Survey of Children India fact sheet (Provisional).* Retrieved from http://wcd.nic.in/issnip/National_Fact%20sheet_RSOC%20_02-07-2015.pdf

Mogudu, H. R., Kumar, M., & Millet, C. (2012). State and socio-demographic group variation in out-of-pocket expenditure, borrowings and Janani Suraksha Yojana (JSY) programme use for birth deliveries in India. *BMC Public Health, 12*, 1048.

Montgomery, A. L, Ram, U., Kumar, R., Jha, P., for The Million Death Study Collaborators. (2014). Maternal Mortality in India: Causes and Healthcare Service Use Based on a Nationally Representative Survey. *PLoS ONE, 9*(1), e83331. https://doi.org/10.1371/journal.pone.0083331

Morrison, J., Thapa, R., Hartley, S., Osrin, D., Manandhar, M., Tumbahangphe, K., ... Costello, A. (2010). Understanding how women's groups improve maternal and newborn health in Makwanpur, Nepal: A qualitative study. *International Health, 2*(1), 25–35.

Nasir, R. (2014). Muslim self exclusion and public health services in Delhi. *South Asia Review, 34*(1), 65–86.

National Health Systems Resource Centre, Government of India. (2011). *Programme evaluation of the Janani Suraksha Yojana.*

Pinto, S. (2006). More than a Dai: Birth, work and rural Dalit women's perspectives. In R. Rawat (Ed.), *Seminar: Special Issue, Dalit Perspectives*, no. 558. New Delhi, India.

Press Information Bureau, Government of India. (2013). Rs. 10456.25 cr Approved for JSY Since its Launch-Ministry of Health and Family Welfare [Press release]. Retrieved from http://pib.nic.in/newsite/PrintRelease.aspx?relid=108540.

Ranadive, B., San Sebastian, M., De Costa, A., & Lindholm, L. (2014). Inequalities in institutional delivery uptake and maternal mortality reduction in the context of cash incentive program, Janani Suraksha Yojana: Results from nine states in India. *Social Science and Medicine, 123*, 1–6.

Registrar General of India. (2006). *Maternal Mortality in India: 1997–2003 Trends, Causes and Risk Factors* Registrar General/Centre for Global Health Research, University of Toronto.

Rowen, T., Prata, N., & Passano, P. (2009). Evaluation of a traditional birth attendant training programme in Bangladesh. *Midwifery, 2*, 229–236.

Tripathy, P., Nair, N., Barnett, S., Mahapatra, R., Borghi, J., Rath, S., ...Costello, A. (2010). Effect of a participatory intervention with women's groups on birth outcomes and maternal depression in Jharkhand and Orissa, India: A cluster-randomised controlled trial. *Lancet, 375*(9721), 1182–1192.

United Nations Population Fund. (2009). *Concurrent assessment of Janani Suraksha Yojana (JSY) in selected states.* New Delhi, India: United Nations Population Fund India.

Vikram, K., Sharma, A. K., & Kannan, T. (2013). Beneficiary level factors influencing Janani Suraksha Yojana utilization in urban slum population of trans-Yamuna area of Delhi. *Indian Journal of Medical Research*, *138*, 340–346.

ABHIJIT DAS is director of Centre for Health and Social Justice at New Delhi, India.

NEW DIRECTIONS FOR EVALUATION • DOI: 10.1002/ev

Solar, O. & Frenz, P. (2017). Lessons from Chile's use of system-level theory of change to implement a policy redesign process to address health inequities. In S. Sridharan, K. Zhao, & A. Nakaima (Eds.), *Building Capacities to Evaluate Health Inequities: Some Lessons Learned from Evaluation Experiments in China, India and Chile. New Directions for Evaluation, 154,* 101–113.

8

Lessons from Chile's Use of System-Level Theory of Change to Implement a Policy Redesign Process to Address Health Inequities

Orielle Solar, Patricia Frenz

Abstract

To reduce health inequities, Chile's Ministry of Health embarked on an ambitious process to implement policy redesign involving six public health programs that used a system-level theory of change. The process brought together a large and diverse group of national and local actors from within and outside the health sector organized in a network of program nodes, who worked together on well-defined tasks over the course of a year with high-level political and technical support. The tasks were part of a coconstructed stepwise assessment methodology, based on understanding and testing program theory and uncovering theories of inequities, drawing on realistic evaluation approaches, the social determinants of health framework, and models of effective program coverage. Almost simultaneously, the program nodes proposed new program theories to address equities with an implementation strategy, which necessarily engaged other sectors and community actors. This chapter highlights some of the lessons to explain the success of Chile's redesign process: (a) the diversity of knowledge and experiences across nodes enriched and enabled system-level change, (b) the key distinction between theory of change and theory of inequities required to address inequities, and (c) the long-lasting transformative capital for institutional change of training a network of agents for change. © 2017 Wiley Periodicals, Inc., and the American Evaluation Association.

NEW DIRECTIONS FOR EVALUATION, no. 154, Summer 2017 © 2017 Wiley Periodicals, Inc., and the American Evaluation Association.   Published online in Wiley Online Library (wileyonlinelibrary.com) • DOI: 10.1002/ev.20246

B etween 2008 and 2010, the Ministry of Health of Chile embarked on a large national experiment in theory-driven evaluation to redesign six public health programs aimed at enhancing equity, as part of several complementary, transformative initiatives of the Steps toward Equity in Health Agenda.

The systemic scope, the focus on inequities, and the effort to produce real-world action almost simultaneously are novel aspects of the Chilean program review and redesign process, going beyond most program evaluations that emphasize a focus on a singular program. In this chapter, we discuss some of the lessons learned from Chile's attempts at using a system-level theory of change to implement a policy redesign process to address health inequities.

The Chilean Policy Context

Chile is an unequal society, shaped by dramatic political and policy shifts over the last decades. Subsequently, it is often cited as a model for policy innovations of radically different types (Ceballos, 2008). For example, the dual legacy of a national health service, established in the 1950s, and the imposition of a private health insurance market during the military dictatorship configured its complex health system of public and private insurance and health care provision (Jimenez de la Jara & Bossert, 1995; Mardones-Restat & de Azevedo, 2006). Increasingly, after the return to democracy in 1990, the thrust of social and health policies emphasizes fulfilling rights. Initially, policy responses focused on minimum standards of social protection for the poorest families, "Chile Solidario" (Chile in Solidarity) but gradually have been moving toward progressive universalism, exemplified in the early child development system, "Chile Crece Contigo" (Chile Grows with You). Nevertheless, social inequities are profound and remain largely unremitting in Chile, reflected in income inequalities with a Gini coefficient of 0.50 and a gap 26.5 times larger for the richest 10% in relation to the poorest 10%, which is substantially greater than the Organisation for Economic Co-operation and Development (OECD, 2014) average of 0.31 and 9.5, respectively. This context has generated social discontent, fuelling social mobilization and, consequently, driving new policy commitments and responses to advance equity.

The Policy Redesign Process

In 2008, the Ministry of Health set out a "Steps Toward Equity in Health Agenda" to reinforce efforts to reduce health inequities through action on the social determinants of health, following the recommendations of the World Health Organization (WHO) Commission on the Social Determinants of Health (Vega, 2011). The agenda encompassed a group of initiatives aimed at strengthening professional and institutional capacities to

Figure 8.1. Node Network Structure for the Policy Redesign Process

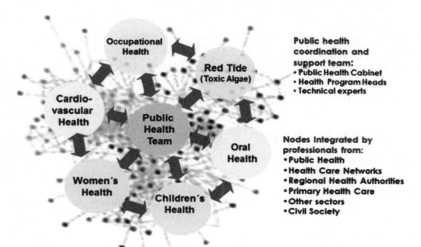

develop intersectoral and participatory policy action, inequality monitoring, and evaluation. One of the steps was a national-level activity to redesign public health programs to address health inequities.

Six health programs of different types, ranging from a primary care cardiovascular health program, to an environmental Red Tide control program, worked together to develop a process of review and redesign aimed at identifying specific program interventions and leveraging health system transformation and engagement of other sectors to better address socially determined health inequities. The process brought together hundreds of actors comprising a diverse group of national program managers, regional and local providers, and civil social and intersectoral partners, organized in a network of program review nodes, backed and supported by the highest political and technical levels of the Ministry of Health (Ministerio de Salud, Chile, 2010a; Ministerio de Salud, Chile, 2010b). A space and structure were created to build connections between nodes and within and outside the health sector to facilitate the type of system-level change required to address health inequities (Figure 8.1).

Collectively, the nodes developed a stepwise methodology to assess—in contrast to its theory—how the programs worked in practice, for whom and under what circumstances and, importantly, who was left behind and why (Sridharan, 2012; Sridharan & Nakaima, 2011; Tanahashi, 1978; WHO, 2008). The methodology incorporated elements from theory-driven evaluative thinking, particularly realistic evaluation, the social determinants of health framework, and models of effective coverage (Pawson & Tilley, 2004; Solar & Irwin, 2010).

The undertaking was synergistic with other initiatives of the Equity Agenda, such as advanced training and capacity building of public health staff for social determinants work and the redress of barriers to health and social services in 169 vulnerable communities, using participatory and intersectorial approaches (WHO, 2011). Capacity building, technical support, and political backing were critical enablers of the process, allowing review teams to carry out the assessment and almost simultaneously develop a redesign proposal and implementation strategy (Vega, 2011).

System-Level Theory of Change to Address Inequities

The method developed by the nodes for the redesign of public health programs considered that all interventions are based on a theory, but the underlying theory is often not explicitly understood, especially if it has not been overtly and clearly described. Thus, the theory needs to be brought to the surface through a reflective process involving stakeholders. Then, the theory is tested to see what happens in practice, by systematically considering who benefits and who is left behind and analyzing barriers beyond the organization of the health care system, such as those associated with the social conditions of life and work of the population. It then necessitates implementing measures to remedy these coverage gaps, acting on the mechanisms generating inequities in collaboration with communities, other sectors, and across health system functions.

The reflective process across nodes—and not just singular programs—the need to engage other actors within and beyond the health sector to redress the theory of inequities, necessarily implies changes at the system level.

Figure 8.2 captures the steps of the methodology, highlighting the evolution of the understanding of the program's theory in the course of the review and redesign process. The initial theory is uncovered and articulated in the first step, which seeks to understand the conceptual basis of the program and how it considers equity. This is a key transformative step because stakeholders usually consider only program objectives or goals and consider equity in relation to targeting program actions for the poorest and most vulnerable, without examining the causes of the causes of inequities. Steps two and three entail testing the theory. Using a theory-driven process, each of the nodes identified the people who are not accessing or receiving the benefits and the barriers or facilitators of access faced by this social group.

With these inputs, in step four the node analyzed the causes of people being left behind and the barriers, uncovering the underlying theory of inequities related to the program. This was done by first identifying the socioeconomic position of the social groups left behind in relation to gender, education, income, social class or ethnicity, and the distribution of power. This meant how they live in relation to material resources, prestige,

Figure 8.2. Theory of System-Level Change to Address Health Inequalities

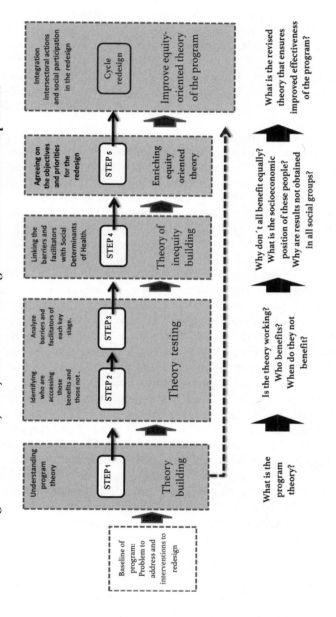

and discrimination in the society. At the same time, the node also examined associations of barriers and facilitators with social determinants of health and "the causes of the causes" of health inequities and position in the social structure. At this point, the nodes were able to identify the influence and role of the other sectors and policies in the generation and amelioration of health inequities. Through this analysis, each of the nodes generated learning that overcoming health inequities is possible only if the multiple programs also look at policies outside of the health sector. The outcome and value-added nature of the process was the framing of an improved, equity-oriented, system-level program theory to be implemented in the program redesign.

Based on the findings from the review and this new program theory, program managers and node members set priorities and objectives for the redesign/reorientation phase; defined which excluded groups must be considered; identified the key programmatic stages in which action could generate greater equity gains; ascertained service barriers and facilitating factors, as well as social determinants in relation to these; and defined mechanisms and opportunities to work with other sectors and ensured participation in order to safeguard health equity and universal coverage.

In the Chilean experience, the nodes found in general that health programs, as originally conceived, did not consider a theory of inequities in health in the construction and implementation. Most public health programs are often built from a biomedical logic, excluding the strong evidence of the social basis of the health-disease process and ignoring the role or influence of social and economic policies. In general, primary prevention of disease is not the priority of the biomedical health model, which focuses on curative care. When the aim of the biomedical model is to "reduce morbidity and premature mortality" (Naidoo & Willis, 2016, p. 76), the focus is on individual lifestyles and behaviors, stressing personal responsibility without considering social patterning and context in the development of a theory of inequities. The theory of social inequities of health is about more than the inclusion of objectives or targets for health equity; it involves the reflection by program managers and implementers about why and how health inequities are generated by their program. By creating spaces for varieties of policy and programmatic stakeholders to interact, the process described in this chapter focused on building robust theories to tackle inequities related to the program.

Redesign of the Red Tide Program

Examining the changes developed by the Red Tide Program shows how the stepwise analysis and the nodal approach contributed to program redesign to address inequities.

Figure 8.3. Initial Red Tide Program Theory

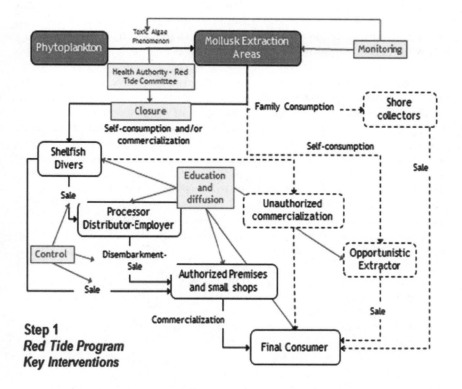

Step 1
Red Tide Program
Key Interventions

A quick look at some of the review and redesign elements of the National Program of Control and Prevention of Poisoning for Harmful Algal Blooms (Red Tide) illustrates the potential usefulness of the Chilean stepwise analysis and redesign for system-level policy change, involving national and local levels and integration of other sectors.

The Red Tide Program aimed to prevent intoxication of the population derived from the consumption of shellfish contaminated by harmful algal bloom (HAB), through the development of four component interventions: monitoring of harvesting areas, education and diffusion, control and surveillance of products prior to consumption, and Red Tide Committee.

The program diagram (Figure 8.3) shows the complexity of contextual influences and potential consequences of the program interventions on the livelihood of certain groups.

The program theory had considered that the actions of monitoring toxic algae and bans to fish in contaminated extraction areas produced public health benefits for the general population by preventing disability and death. It was deemed successful because no deaths had been registered in recent years, only cases of gastroenteritis disease. However, when the Red

Tide node examined the inequities related to the program, considering different actors and the productive chain, they became aware of important social and economic impacts on fishing communities when the prohibition of extraction was decreed. Previously, the health program ignored the concerns of fishing communities and their families and the equity impact was unaddressed.

However, before acting, the node considered that more information was needed. Accordingly, the national program managers, working closely with regional-level managers in the affected areas of the country, decided to investigate and measure the specific socioeconomic impacts of health actions prohibiting extraction, particularly on poorer artisan fishers and their families. The complexity of influences had to be addressed in designing the policy solution, requiring the participation of different actors, different levels of public management, and other sectors besides the health sector. In addition, the complexity encompassed consideration of contextual changes essential to advancing the goals of health and social equity.

The results of the study were used to redesign the program, including new redesign objectives and priorities:

- Implementation of Red Tide Committees with intersectoral and social participation at the community or local level (including educational activities and dissemination).
- Characterization of priority groups to quantify the specific economic impacts of the closure measures in different communities. For example, communities with ethnic roots, such as the **Kawéskar (Alacalufe)**, whose subsistence depends almost exclusively on shellfish harvesting, are affected in their living conditions.
- Generation of an intersectoral mitigation plan (social and economic) in the Red Tide Committee. This included national and regional levels of the Ministries of Economy, Social Planning, and Health and the Fisheries Service.
- Changes in the monitoring schemes with community participation, providing timely information to communities of the results of monitoring and outcomes of decision making from the beginning.

The changes introduced in the Red Tide program are illustrated in Figure 8.4.

Evaluation Influences of the Chilean Experience

The evaluative thinking process to review and redesign six public health programs, developed over an 18-month period between 2009 and 2010, exerted lasting influences on the participants as individuals; such influence was spread throughout the review team networks and also resulted in collective changes for the programs and the Ministry of Health and Regional

Figure 8.4. Revised Red Tide Program

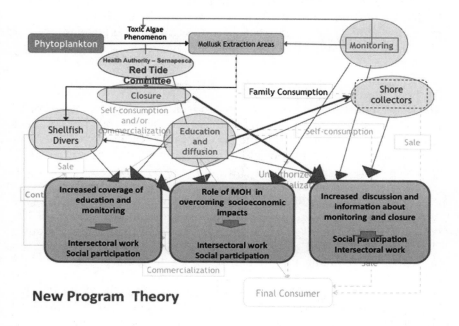

Health Authorities. A new initiative after 2010 was developed from regional nodes and authorities and included qualitative studies to collect perceptions of members of the Red Tide communities.

The participants gained new attitudes and understanding of the salience of health equity and skills, developed by doing, and primed through organized training. Interpersonal relations across health programs, between levels, and with intersectoral and civil society actors deepened, through interaction and understanding of common goals. From all the intersectoral work and social participation came constitutive pillars of each program. These common interests were the basis for persuading other sectors to work collaboratively.

The investment in the process resulted in a new generation of agents for change in the public health sector, at all levels, in addition to players in other sectors. Organizational commitment to equity was embedded in the new health objectives and strategies for the 2011–2020 decade. Equity became a necessary aspect of policy-oriented learning and policy change. It built a consensus about the importance of the social aspects in the program and how the health sector has a responsibility around this.

Not all of the reorientation work was sustained in subsequent years, because of government changes and changes in priorities, but what was sustained were the connections among the different stakeholders around

NEW DIRECTIONS FOR EVALUATION • DOI: 10.1002/ev

evaluative thinking to develop collaborative and integrated policies to address inequities. This often continued at the regional and local levels to further innovation for equity. There was a greater sense that policy implementation should be a coconstructed process that requires adaptation to the diverse cultural context that exists within Chile.

Global Uptake and Conclusions

The value of the Chilean experience is also seen in its global uptake. Around the world, national health programs are striving to ensure that "no one is left behind." In 2010 and 2011, and drawing on the Chilean work, the Ministry of Health, Equity and Social Policy of Spain applied the reorientation approach in its training process, "Integration of a focus on social determinants of health and health equity into health strategies, programs and activities at national and autonomous community levels." The approach served to review nine health programs and propose reorientations for them. The reorientation methodology was adapted by the WHO in its Innov8 resource after piloting in several countries: a multicountry effort in Europe to improve maternal child health program access for the Roma people, to reduce gaps in reproductive and neonatal health in Indonesia, and to strengthen equity in the adolescent sexual health program of Nepal and in the diabetes program in Morocco (WHO, 2016). At present, Chile's Ministry of Health is again developing review and redesign processes to reinvigorate its health promotion program toward an equity-oriented health-in-all-policies approach.

Equity is not about a single program but requires partnership across a diverse set of actors to find and address solutions. Thus, the diversity of knowledge and experiences of a variety of players is key to the success of a system-level redesign process; diverse stakeholders participated in each node, including professionals from different programs and sectors, whereas contributions of civil society were crucial in some of the nodes. The interaction across different nodes helped unpack the diversity and complexity of the process.

One of our learnings was that a distinction needs to be made between a theory of change and a theory of inequities. Not all redesigned policy interventions lead to greater equity in results. The effectiveness or cost effectiveness of intervention does not necessarily translate into improvements for all social groups. To ensure that policy changes benefit all social groups, the Chilean nodes learned that changes in the program must respond to the diversity of needs of various groups, i.e., it must recognize the heterogeneity of program participants and their differential needs. Second, the program must consider in which context it is working or will be applied and whether or not it is possible to implement the proposed changes. Third, the role and influence of diversity of actors and sectors must be recognized as necessary to produce change. All of these aspects involve taking into account the complexity of taking action on inequities. In essence, we learned that understanding why the inequities exist in the program is at the center of change; so uncovering the theory of inequities of the program could shed light on which interventions could address inequities.

The commitment and engagement of the node members were facilitated by the process of coconstruction of the review and redesign methodology. Adaptations and creativity are required to build a participatory and reflective process.

One of the results of this process is the creation of a new generation of agents for change in the public health sector. This is especially important because transformative processes are often based on nonlinear changes. Sometimes there are advances and then retreats. The important thing is to be able to identify windows of opportunities and to align problems with solutions by counting on the capacities to act off agents for change.

Chile's novel theory-driven evaluation intervention to integrate equity into health programs developed in 2009–2010 and has been taken further forward globally and nationally, generating many lessons as discussed throughout the chapter. Salient among them are:

- The program review and redesign methodology is a *learning by doing* process, which optimally should be done in parallel with capacity building of staff through training courses, including evaluation workshops, within a broader strategy to integrate equity into health system duties and practice.
- The Chilean process was not heavily constrained by lack of availability of information on inequities. Scarcity of data was overcome by gathering and testing local practices, by commissioning specific studies and, most important, by ensuring a strong monitoring and evaluation plan for the implemented changes.
- The challenge in addressing inequities is that interventions, which are effective on the average, may be ineffective in reducing inequities. This means that bold and innovative approaches are required, whose effectiveness for overall average improvement and inequities must be tested.
- Time is needed to see results, but at the same time it is necessary to develop process and outcome indicators for monitoring in the short term, to share advances with authorities and stakeholders, leverage commitment and resources, and make adjustments if progress is off track.
- Context matters. Adaptation of programs to national and local contexts is essential. Adaptation of this methodology to different contexts is also important.
- The Universal Health Coverage/health system strengthening dimensions of the reorientation process needs to be robust, particularly to make sure that vertical programs are not analyzed in isolation, without interaction across levels and other programs, an aspect addressed by the node structure.

- Effectively addressing the growing urgency of health and social equity in national and global agendas, exemplified by the 2030 Sustainable Development Goals (United Nations, 2015), requires novel approaches that will be further enhanced through sharing experiences and best practices.
- The mantra of an effective health system should be: A program can be successful only "when it is at least as effective for the lowest socioeconomic status groups as for the highest" (Petticrew & MacIntyre, 2001, p. 55).

References

Ceballos, M. A. (2008). Chile: un caso latinoamericano de política social post-ajustes estructurales. *Nuevo Mundo Mundos Nuevos* [online]. Retrieved from http://nuevomundo.revues.org/11212. https://doi.org/10.4000/nuevomundo.11212

Jimenez de la Jara, J., & Bossert, T. (1995). Chile's health sector reform: Lessons from four reform periods. *Health Policy*, 32(1–3), 155–166. Retrieved from http://linkinghub.elsevier.com/retrieve/pii/0168851095007339

Mardones-Restat, F., & de Azevedo, A. C. (2006). The essential health reform in Chile; a reflection on the 1952 process. *Salud pública de México*, 48(6), 504–511. Retrieved from http://www.ncbi.nlm.nih.gov/pubmed/17326347

Ministerio de Salud, Chile. (2010a). *Documento Técnico I: Pauta para Iniciar la Revisión de los Programas: Lista de Chequeo de Equidad. Serie de Documentos Técnicos del Rediseño de los Programas desde la Perspectiva de Equidad y Determinantes Sociales.* Santiago: Subsecretaría de Salud Pública [Technical document II for supporting the review and redesign of public health programmes from the perspective of equity and social determinants of health. Santiago: Undersecretary for Public Health.]

Ministerio de Salud, Chile. (2010b). *Documento Técnico II, III: Serie de Documentos Técnicos del Rediseño de los Programas desde la Perspectiva de Equidad y Determinantes Sociales.* Santiago: Subsecretaría de Salud Pública. [Technical documents I, II and III for supporting the review and redesign of public health programmes from the perspective of equity and social determinants of health. Santiago: Undersecretary for Public Health.]

Naidoo, J., & Wills, J. (2016). *Foundations for health promotion* (4th ed.). Amsterdam, The Netherlands: Elsevier.

Organisation for Economic Co-operation and Development. (2014). *Society at a glance 2014 highlights: Chile OECD social indicators.* Retrieved from https://www.oecd.org/chile/OECD-SocietyAtaGlance2014-Highlights-Chile.pdf

Pawson, R., & Tilley, N. (2004). *Realist evaluation.* London: British Cabinet Office. Retrieved from http://www.communitymatters.com.au/RE_chapter.pdf

Petticrew, M., & Macintyre, S. (2001). What do we know about the effectiveness and cost-effectiveness of measures to reduce inequalities in health? In O. A. Cookson & R. McDaid (Eds.), *Issues panel for equity in health: The discussion papers* (pp. 54–61). London: Nuffield Foundation. Retrieved from https://www.nuffieldtrust.org.uk/files/2017-01/issues-panel-equity-in-health-web-final.pdf

Solar, O., & Irwin, A. (2010). *A conceptual framework for action on the social determinants of health (Social Determinants of Health Discussion Paper 2: Policy and Practice).* Geneva: World Health Organization. Retrieved from http://www.who.int/sdhconference/resources/ConceptualframeworkforactiononSDH_eng.pdf

Sridharan, S. (2012). *A pocket guide to evaluating health equity interventions—Some questions for reflection.* Retrieved from http://www.longwoods.com/blog/a-pocket-guide-to-evaluating-health-equity-interventions-some-questions-for-reflection/

Sridharan, S., & Nakaima, A. (2011). Ten steps to making evaluation matter. *Evaluation and Program Planning, 34*(2), 135–146. Retrieved from http://www.sciencedirect.com/science/article/pii/S0149718910000819

Tanahashi, T. (1978). Health service coverage and its evaluation. *Bulletin of the World Health Organization, 56*(2), 295–303.

United Nations. (2015). SDGs: Sustainable Development Knowledge Platform. Retrieved from https://sustainabledevelopment.un.org/sdgs

Vega, J. (2011). *Steps towards the health equity agenda in Chile.* Draft paper for the for the World Conference on Social Determinants of Health, October 19–21, 2011, Río de Janeiro. Retrieved from http://www.who.int/sdhconference/resources/draft_background_paper25_chile.pdf

World Health Organization. (2008). *Closing the gap in a generation: Health equity through action on the social determinants of health.* Geneva: Author. Retrieved from http://whqlibdoc.who.int/publications/2008/9789241563703_eng.pdf

World Health Organization (2011). *Rio Political Declaration on Social Determinants of Health.* Retrieved from http://www.who.int/sdhconference/declaration/Rio_political_declaration.pdf?ua=1

World Health Organization (2016). *The Innov8 approach for reviewing national health programmes to leave no one behind.* Retrieved from http://www.who.int/life-course/partners/innov8/innov8-technical-handbook/en/

ORIELLE SOLAR is the research director of the health equity and employment program at the Facultad Latinoamericana de Ciencias Sociales (FLACSO) Chile.

PATRICIA FRENZ is associate professor and research director at the School of Public Health, Faculty of Medicine, University of Chile.

Carden, F. (2017). Building evaluation capacity to address problems of equity. In S. Sridharan, K. Zhao, & A. Nakaima (Eds.), *Building Capacities to Evaluate Health Inequities: Some Lessons Learned from Evaluation Experiments in China, India and Chile. New Directions for Evaluation, 154*, 115–125.

9

Building Evaluation Capacity to Address Problems of Equity

Fred Carden

Abstract

The issue of equity is receiving increasing attention not only in health but in other areas of social development. It is often a highly charged and emotional conversation. This chapter argues that with better capacity to evaluate for equity, evaluators can make a significant contribution to clarifying the issues in the debate and, through that, to addressing inequities. Evidence is never the only element in a debate—politics and emotion always play important roles—but the absence of solid evidence fosters even stronger polarization of the debate. This chapter addresses a gap in our capacity to evaluate for equity so that evidence can make a central contribution to this debate. Building on the challenges to measurement in the equity space, the chapter identifies the process and systems thinking skills that are needed to complement our evaluation methods skills. © 2017 Wiley Periodicals, Inc., and the American Evaluation Association.

E quity is receiving increasing attention in social programs. Less attention is paid to its evaluation and the capacities to evaluate it: in a scoping review, the authors found that the literature focused more on describing individual programs and less on the effectiveness of the strategies at play; and in that review, equity was not mentioned (Hotte et al., 2015). Some mention equity (Raynor, 2014) but do not elaborate on how it should be considered. Others (Bamberger & Segone, 2013) talk about designing evaluation for equity but not about how to effectively build capacities to do so; they note that, "so far, the evaluation literature only provides emerging guidance on how to evaluate outcomes and impacts for these kinds of complex interventions" (p. 31). The "how" is the critical question for evaluators. This chapter explores this challenge and proposes some core elements to capacities for equity evaluation.

Michael Patton (2003) observed that, "evaluation is too valuable and scarce a resource to be wasted just producing reports" (p. viii). This chapter explores evaluation capacity through that lens. Building evaluation capacity is not only about tools and methods to conduct evaluation to produce reports but also about capacities to promote the use of evaluation and capacities to focus on how evaluation contributes to improvement in social programs. These capacities take on even more importance when we focus on problems of equity and evaluation that can contribute both to our understanding of how inequities can unwittingly get built into programs and point to some potential solutions.

The capacities to evaluate are more than technical; they are sociotechnical (Trist, 1981). Sociotechnical systems build on a redundancy of functions rather than a redundancy of parts. This capacity to take on more than one specialized task increases the flexibility and adaptive capacities of a system. In other words, in addition to the technical capacities to undertake a methodologically sound evaluation, there are social capacities to engage effectively with the evaluand, capacities to communicate, to persuade, and to enable a deeper understanding of the social change contributions that evaluation can make. This entails a shift from the perspective of expert decision maker to an engagement model. Other aspects of building capacities to evaluate equity include the importance of context and the need to situate equity evaluation in its setting rather than exclusively within the intervention. As Oumoul Ba Tall (2009) said, in responding to a discussion at the European Evaluation Society Conference "it is not about your project, it is about my country." The next few sections explore what these issues mean for building capacity to evaluate equity.

Problems of Equity

As Bamberger and Segone (2013) note, international commitments can be realized only through a much greater emphasis on equity among and within regions and countries. Equity, unlike equality, is not easily measured. Both refer to fairness and justice, but equality can be easily enumerated because of its implications of sameness. Equity, on the other hand, has a major normative element that is focused on equivalence not sameness. It requires taking account of context and of individual situations in ways equality does not have to consider (McSherry, 2013). This is a critical distinction for evaluation because it means that the average state of a society does not tell us anything about equity within that society. Evaluation cannot rely on national or regional data but must find ways to obtain a finer grained understanding of how equity is playing out within communities and in social relations, particularly with marginalized groups. It must do so while dealing with a normative concept that cannot be easily reduced to empirical data.

Equity remains a concept under definition and redefinition. Whitehead (1992) defines equity as differences that are unjust, unfair, and avoidable. This leads to problems of measurement as concepts of justice and fairness are rooted in culture and context. They are normative concepts and mean different things in different societies and among groups with different values. In an attempt to begin to address this, Braveman and Gruskin (2003) refine the definition as "the absence of systematic disparities ... between more and less advantaged social groups" (p. 258). This does not remove the measurement problem completely because equity remains an ethical value, inherently normative and grounded in the principle of distributive justice.

Distributive justice raises additional questions. It is about the idea of a fair process of exchange and engagement, but as Capp, Savage, and Clarke (2001) note, that raises ethical questions: in an environment of constrained resources, how do you decide to spend money on medical equipment that will serve one population (cardiac patients) but which purchase also means that resources will be unavailable for other illnesses or for preventative treatments? The principles behind distributive justice range from libertarian to egalitarian (Stanford Encyclopedia of Philosophy, 1996), which means that clarity about the values and perspectives of those involved are essential. Without that, very different understandings of what constitutes distributive justice will be at play. Capp et al. (2001) noted that in their experience, the discussion was not had and decisions were taken in a political manner.

Österle (2002) argues that there are four sets of equity objectives: (a) guaranteeing minimum standards, (b) supporting living standards, (c) reducing inequality, and (d) promoting social integration. Of these, the first three address quantitative dimensions (money, access to services, and comparison to a threshold). The fourth is based on values and context and is much more difficult to measure. Different people and different groups may interpret what it means in competing ways. The normative dimension suggests capacity for clarity in design and evaluation.

The concept of equity is fundamentally political. Its normative nature means that equity is socially constructed and reflective of the views of a society. At the same time, it is closely aligned to human rights. As such, fundamental inequities that may be seen as just in some societies (i.e., role of women; position of individuals with disabilities in society; racial differences) can also be assessed against principles of human rights even where the context denies the existence of inequity.

Problems of equity, or more precisely inequity, haunt many interventions designed to contribute to improving society. In spite of our best intentions, too often interventions do not reach the target audience. Our ability to measure progress has been hindered by a number of factors, which are outlined next. The issue of meaning and definition in understanding equity poses significant challenges for evaluation. Clarity is essential for measurement, especially for hard-to-measure areas. The methods we tend to use and that drive the evaluation of much development programming have several dimensions that make it hard for them to highlight and assess inequities.

Problems of Evaluation

Before discussing capacity building for equity, it is important to summarize the key challenges that evaluation faces when attempting to confront equity.

Averages Mask Inequity

Much evaluation focuses on the whole community so it comes up with averages that demonstrate progress (or not). This hides inequities within the community under treatment and investigation. Have a Heart Paisley, a program to reach the poorest members of a community with improved health care programs, found in its evaluation that the program was making a difference (Blamey et al., 2004; Sridharan et al., 2008). A closer look at the data showed, however, that the program was failing to reach their real target audience, the most vulnerable members of the community. This is a common occurrence because too often we fail to adequately segment the treatment group to identify who is benefitting and who is not. We are looking for the total change so we look at the totals. This is compounded by a search for impact rather than a search for why and under what conditions impact is achieved.

The Intervention May Be the Wrong Unit of Analysis to Understand Equity

Evaluation tends to look at specific projects and programs. The funder wants to know how the project is working and whether or not it is meeting its objectives. Evaluation methods therefore have developed largely around looking at projects and programs and have been less aware of defining the problem at the level of the community, organization, or institution within which the intervention is taking place. The risk is that it is easier to miss seeing what the intervention is doing wrong if we look only at the intervention without considering other factors and intervening variables that meant that although the individual intervention achieved its objectives, it either failed to contribute to a better condition or indeed made the condition worse. Describing this in an examination of organizational assessment of development organizations, Lusthaus, Adrien, Anderson, Carden, & Plinio Montalván (2002) note, "They can become trapped by their own success and stand at risk of serious organizational decline" (p. 164).

Priority to Funder Outcomes Distorts Evaluation

When the funder is not part of the community, it has its own priorities and must respond to its governance body concerning the success of its funding. It measures against its own criteria. There is a potential for distortion in this process when the priorities of the funder do not match the priorities in the community that is being served—as Ba Tall (2009), referenced earlier in this chapter, noted "it is not about your project, it is about my country."

The Professionalization of Evaluation Removes Checks and Balances

Somewhat ironically the professionalization of evaluation has often removed the business of assessment from the day-to-day management of programs and organizations where it belongs. By handing it to a small group of experts, managers tend to leave it to the professionals when in fact engagement is essential to good evaluation. Consequently, evaluators have isolated themselves rather than serving as an integral part of the management team. Evaluation capacity then is not something to be isolated in a small group but is needed throughout a system; and those who lead an evaluation need the skills not only for good methodological work but also to help strengthen the whole organization's use of evaluative thinking (Carden & Earl, 2007). Full engagement leads to a deeper understanding not only of outcomes but also at the mechanisms at play—how and in what contexts these outcomes are achieved.

An Outcome Focus Often Hides Process

In recent years, there has been a big push in evaluation to focus on outcomes and impacts. What is often lost in this approach is a better understanding of the processes and mechanisms that led to the outcomes and impacts: what actually happened and to whom, leading up to the outcomes that were achieved? This is where we can learn more about what works, for whom, and in what context and thereby have the opportunity to apply the lessons in new settings.

There Is a Tendency to Focus on Only What Is Measurable

Measuring change is difficult. After Österle (2002), the fourth equity objective of promoting social integration is not easily measured. It is based on values and context and these do not lend themselves easily to quick and simple measurement tools. Measuring in this space calls for a deep understanding of context as well as clarification of the values of both those who fund the intervention and those who engage in the intervention as clients or interveners.

The capacity to evaluate needs to take into account the hard-to-measure and the intangibles. It is equally clear, that it is not only about measuring the intangibles. There are many tangible and measurable aspects to equity around standard of living across a society, levels of inequality/equality in a society. But if we restrict ourselves to what is easily measured we will miss critical factors related to equity.

Evaluation Capacity for Equity—Moving to Solution Spaces

In a review of impact evaluation and a challenge to the prevalence of one model for evaluating impact, the IE4D Group (Rogers et al., 2001) wrote a paper in which they used the framework of "rethink, reshape, reform" to discuss impact evaluation and how it could evolve. There is no singular model for addressing equity evaluation. As in any evaluation, form should follow function. That is, the "best" method for evaluating equity is going to depend on the context, available data, the question one is trying to answer and the resources available. Building capacity to evaluate equity means building capacities to rethink evaluation practice away from the project to the system; reshape evaluation to be more scientific (theory based) and able to explain process; and the capacities to use this new knowledge to reform evaluation practice to more effectively contribute not only to measuring inequities but to doing something about them. And as I outline in this section, the process of rethink, reshape, reform is incomplete because the process is an ongoing and iterative one, not a one-time reform process. So, rethink, reshape, reform capacity for equity evaluation; but then review and revise again.

Rethink

As the IE4D Group noted, rethinking evaluation is about considering how it supports or undermines self-determination and improved results in the long term. If we take a long-term perspective, the implication is that the intervention itself is the wrong unit of analysis as noted earlier in this chapter. The unit of analysis should be the system in which the intervention occurs. Here we refer to capacities to focus on the system first rather than on the intervention itself. This is particularly important for equity evaluation because in order to understand the effect of an intervention on an individual (particularly a social intervention) it is critical to look beyond the individual in relation to the intervention and understand how, for different members of a society, that intervention has improved or worsened the welfare of the community and its different members. Systems-level analysis is a burgeoning field that has not sufficiently touched evaluation in use. Although a number of new evaluation approaches and tools take a systems perspective in their design (developmental evaluation; Patton, 2011), outcome mapping (Earl, Carden, & Smutylo, 2001) to name but two and there is an increasing emphasis in systems approaches to the adaptation and use of other methods as well as the development of new methods (Williams & Imam, 2004, among others), the majority of evaluations commissioned are still focused on the interests of the funder in the intervention under question, so the application of methods is compromised by the narrow focus on the solution, the funder has identified and supported rather than its interaction with the context.

Systems-level evaluation means that accountability is to the community in all its diversity, not primarily to the funder of the intervention. It further means that transparency across interventions is important. It also includes analysis across multiple data sets, a skill that Davidson (2014) notes is weak; there is a generally agreed priority to the importance of both quantitative and qualitative data, but a generally weak capacity to synthesize analysis across these diverse data sets. This leads us to a reshaping of evaluation around a more science-based approach.

Reshape

Evaluation is in many respects treated as a series of tools to be applied according to the discretion of the funder or, sometimes, the evaluator. Treating it as a science (Pawson, 2013) has a number of implications. Theories in science are a causal explanation for the effects of an intervention and for the effects by the interaction of multiple interventions. This means searching for patterns and rules that can help us understand. As such, theories are not unique to every intervention. Rather, theories tend to cut across multiple interventions and are an explanation of why when something is added to something else, a certain reaction occurs. So there are commonalities across interventions; but science can also help to distinguish unique features in how an intervention works in different settings. Theories are also meant to evolve as we learn.

This is the basis for the "theory of change" approach in evaluation. However, theory of change as applied has two major problems. First, it tends to focus on the singular intervention rather than taking advantage of its scientific foundation and linking to other interventions. Second, it is too often honored in the breach and developed after the intervention is designed to make the funding case rather than explicating the theory in advance—and linking it to other theories of change. The first point means that each theory of change is uniquely developed rather than identifying other experiences using that theory and building on it. As a result, there is a great deal of repetition of errors and relearning of lessons, all at significant expense. There are no mechanisms to track the theories in use and the effects in particular cases, so that first the learning can be used by others in planning interventions but also so that the learning can improve the theory (or indeed disprove it).

The second important point noted about theories of change is that as they are increasingly required by funding agencies, they are more and more honored in the breach, developed to defend an idea rather than as the starting point for designing an intervention. This is linked to pressures for funding, pressure on timelines and a lack of access to a bank of information on similar interventions and how these have played out over time. The theory of change should not be seen as a tool for achieving intervention approval but as the guiding influence in the original design.

Weak theory is susceptible to cognitive bias (House, 2014). Biases such as confirmation bias, group think, and how we deal with conflict of interest all come into play when theory is weak. Equity evaluation is particularly susceptible to weak theory guiding evaluation because of its complexity and measurement challenges. Capacities to identify the theory and identify other interventions that have used that theory and learn from them is crucial. Given the lack of a database (similar to the Campbell Collaboration), capacities to network and exchange with others who might be using similar theories is important. Capacities to look at processes not only outcomes are important, because it is in processes we are most likely to identify differential impacts in different populations within a community.

Reform

Reforming capacities for equity evaluation is about testing new approaches. It involves a certain amount of trial and error and includes the capacity to fail—the capacity to both accept the risk and learn from the tests.

Capacities for reforming evaluation for equity are capacities to engage and invest in change and capacities to focus on the fine-grained impacts of interventions, not their average contribution. Capacities can be summarized in three key points:

Promote Systems Approaches

- Embed evaluation in management and decision systems, not as a separate specialist function
- Focus on the intervention in context as a key factor in the success of interventions
- Build networks and relationships to create linkages and build trust

Expand Accountabilities

- Develop accountability mechanisms that consider clients as central
- Maintain accountabilities to funding sources

Strengthen Learning Approaches

- Build facilitation and communication skills; use them to reach out to all parties
- Prioritize reflection in your practice and in your organization
- Build technical skills on an ongoing basis

Review

The story does not end with a reform effort no matter how successful. Contexts change and issues evolve. Review needs to be a central capacity in approaches to equity evaluation. As Baretto-Fernandes and Ndiaye (in Earl, Verma, Baretto-Fernandes, Kulkarni, & Pant, 2006) note, "being busy creates a mindset that is not conducive to innovation and creativity. Time to discuss reflect, and generate new ideas is the ransom that [evaluation] demands for innovation" (p. 28). Review is the poor sister to design. It is underresourced and often left to impression and guesswork. Building reflection directly into evaluation efforts is a capacity that will make a major contribution to evaluating equity. Capacities for the facilitation of critical analysis are central here.

Revise

Building a learning approach that helps us evaluate equity means building an understanding of the mechanisms that are at play; why did something happen for this group but not another? In what contexts did it happen? Revising is about the capacities to integrate what we are learning into how we apply our theory of change. It is not the same thing as capturing "lessons learned" (which are often "lessons-not-yet-learned"), as is the most common practice in development evaluation. A robust learning system permits error and integrates the cycle of action from design, through implementation and management, assessment, reporting, and on to redesign for new initiatives. It includes capacities for cycles of reflection at the intervention and system level, as well as tools for documenting and retrieving experience so it can be reused.

Conclusions

Inequity is not inevitable. It is a choice and overcoming it is equally a choice. Equity does not negate the existence of competition and difference in a society. Rather it addresses difference that is unjust, unfair, and avoidable. Evaluation can contribute to addressing inequities by making them evident and by questioning interventions and initiatives from the perspective of who benefits and who does not.

Those who want to evaluate for equity and want to understand how to promote a more equitable society need to be concerned about the fine-grained differences that interventions have for different groups in society. Equally they need the capacities to look at interventions from the perspective of the system in which they are acting.

What equity highlights is the need for much more focus on the specifics, much more clarity of purpose and a stronger understanding of processes not just outcomes.

Evaluation has an important contribution to make to understanding— and addressing—inequity. In order to make that contribution, capacities to evaluate equity need attention. I have argued here that a specific focus on capacity for equity evaluation matters, that it needs to address a range of capacities for evaluation from a systems perspective as well as capacities beyond method skills to process skills. Expanding the conversation about equity with better evidence is the objective of stronger capacities because it is in expanding the conversation that we identify solutions to inequities.

References

Ba Tall, Oumol. (2009). Speaking at the European Evaluation Society Conference.

Bamberger, M., & Segone, M. (2013). *How to design and manage equity-focused evaluations*. New York: UNICEF.

Blamey, A., Ayana, M., Lawson, L., Mackinnon, J., Paterson, I., & Judge, K. (2004). *Final report of the Independent Evaluation of Have a Heart Paisley*. Glasgow, Scotland: University of Glasgow.

Braveman, P., & Gruskin, S. (2003). Defining equity in health. *Journal of Epidemiology and Community Health*, 57, 254–258.

Capp, S., Savage, S., & Clarke, V. (2001). Exploring distributive justice in health care. *Australian Health Review*, 24(1),40–44.

Carden, F. & Earl, S. (2007). Infusing Evaluative Thinking as Process Use: The case of the International Development Research Centre. In *New Directions for Evaluation*, 2007(116), 61–73. https://doi.org/10.1002/ev.243

Davidson, J. (2014). How "beauty" can bring truth and justice to life. In J. C. Griffith & B. Montrosse-Moorhead, *New Directions for Evaluation: No. 142. Revisiting truth, beauty, and justice: Evaluating with validity in the 21st century* (pp. 31–43). San Francisco, CA: Jossey-Bass.

Earl, S., Carden, F., & Smutylo, T. (2001). *Outcome mapping: Building learning and reflection into development programs*. Ottawa, Ontario: International Development Research Centre.

Earl, S., Verma, R., Baretto-Fernandes, T., Kulkarni, S., & Pant, K. (2006). *Outcome mapping: Those who dream make a difference*. Ottawa, Ontario: International Development Research Centre.

Hotte, N., Simmons, L., Beaton, K., & the LCDP Working Group. (2015). *Scoping review of evaluation capacity building strategies*. Cornwall, Ontario, Canada. Retrieved from http://www.eohu.ca/_files/resources/resource1754.pdf

House, E. R. (2014). Origins of the ideas in evaluating with validity. In J. C. Griffith & B. Montrosse-Moorhead, *New Directions for Evaluation: No. 142. Revisiting truth, beauty, and justice: Evaluating with validity in the 21st century* (pp. 9–15). San Francisco, CA: Jossey-Bass.

Lusthaus, C., Adrien, M.-H., Anderson, G., Carden, F., & Plinio Montalván, G. (2002). *Organizational assessment: A framework for improving performance*. Washington, DC: Inter-American Development Bank & Ottawa, Ontario: International Development Research Centre.

McSherry, B. (2013). *What is social equity*. Melbourne, Australia: University of Melbourne, Social Equity Institute. Retrieved from www.socialequity.unimelb.edu.au/What-is-social-equity/.

Österle, A. (2002). Evaluating equity in social policy: A framework for comparative analysis. *Evaluation*, 8(1), 46–59.

Patton, M. Q. (2003). Foreword. In D. Horton et al., *Evaluating capacity development: Experiences from research and development organizations around the world* (pp. v–viii). The Hague, The Netherlands: International Service for National Agricultural Research (ISNAR); Ottawa, Ontario: International Development Research Centre (IDRC); Wageningen, The Netherlands: ACP-EU Technical Centre for Agricultural and Rural Co-operation (CTA).

Patton, M. Q. (2011). *Developmental evaluation: Applying complexity concepts to enhance innovation and use.* New York: Guilford.

Pawson, R. (2013). *The science of evaluation.* Thousand Oaks, CA: Sage.

Raynor, J. (2014, November 19). The return of capacity building. *Stanford Social Innovation Review.*

Rogers, P., Bonbright, D., Earl, S., Ofir, Z., Khagram, S. & McPherson, N. (2011). Impact Evaluation for Development Group. *Impact evaluation for development: Principles for action.* New York: Rockefeller Foundation.

Sridharan, S., Gnich, W., Moffatt, V., Bolton, J., Harkins, C., Hume, M., & Doherty, P. (2008). *Learning from the independent evaluation of Have a Heart Paisley Phase 2, executive summary.* Edinburgh, Scotland: NHS Health Scotland. Retrieved from www.healthscotland.com/uploads/documents/8200-executive_summary_HAHP2.pdf.

Stanford Encyclopedia of Philosophy. (1996). Distributive justice. Retrieved from http://plato.stanford.edu/entries/justice-distributive.

Trist, E. (1981). *The evolution of socio-technical systems* (Issues in the Quality of Working Life, Working Paper 2). Ottawa, Ontario: Ontario Ministry of Labour.

Whitehead, M. (1992). The concepts and principles of equity in health. *International Journal of Health Services, 22,* 429–445.

Williams, B., & Imam, I. (Eds.). (2004). *Systems concepts in evaluation.* Washington, DC: American Evaluation Association.

FRED CARDEN *is founder and principal at Using Evidence Inc.*

Mark, M. M. (2017). Inequities and evaluation influence. In S. Sridharan, K. Zhao, & A. Nakaima (Eds.), *Building Capacities to Evaluate Health Inequities: Some Lessons Learned from Evaluation Experiments in China, India and Chile. New Directions for Evaluation, 154,* 127–138.

10

Inequities and Evaluation Influence

Melvin M. Mark

Abstract

Inspired by a set of evaluators building evaluation capacity in China, India, and Chile, this paper applies a conceptualization of evaluation influence to evaluations and evaluation capacity building related to inequities. © 2017 Wiley Periodicals, Inc., and the American Evaluation Association.

People in different social categories often experience vastly disparate circumstances. We live in a world in which important disparities often exist across subgroups involving race, gender, ethnicity, socioeconomic status, disability status, nationality, intranational location (e.g., region or neighborhood), and so on. Disparities exist on various important aspects of life, including health outcomes, educational attainment and performance, income and wealth, criminal justice outcomes, and more.

Governments, foundations, charities, and other groups often engage in efforts to reduce such disparities, or alternatively, to attenuate their negative effects. In light of such efforts, evaluators need to continue to wrestle with the question: What are the best ways to evaluate programs and other initiatives aimed at disparities? Evaluators also need to wrestle with a companion question: How best can we try to increase the appropriate use and influence of these evaluations? This volume focuses on another related question: How should we increase evaluation capacity regarding social disparities?

Social disparities have received growing attention in recent years among the public, policymakers, and evaluators. In terms of public attention, consider the international response to the best-selling works of Thomas Piketty (2013, 2015). One indicator of interest among policy-makers is the inclusion of several equity-related matters in the Millennium Development Goals, or MDGs (United Nations, 2015). Among evaluators, a growing list of publications addresses the evaluation of initiatives directed at social disparities (e.g., Bamberger & Segone, 2014; Donaldson & Picciotto, 2016; UNICEF, 2012).

The label "inequity" is often used rather than the somewhat sterile term "social disparity." As noted elsewhere in this volume, definitional issues arise when a disparity is judged to be an inequity. In common language, to call a disparity an inequity is to say that the disparity is wrong and should not persist (at least not at its current magnitude). For the most part, if circumstances have reached the point that evaluators are involved, then at least some relevant parties likely view the discrepancy as an inequity. For this reason, I use the terms more or less interchangeably here.

This chapter begins with a brief overarching comment on the work described earlier in this volume. Then comes a brief review of the general approaches evaluators have taken in evaluating inequities. Following that I discuss the possible role of "influence pathways" in evaluation that focus on health (or other) inequities. In addition to health inequities, I make reference to other domains in which disparities and inequities are of interest.

Approaches to the Inequity-Related Evaluation

Rogers (2016) discusses how equity considerations can be incorporated in each of a series of tasks that are undertaken in an evaluation. Alternatively, one can identify different general approaches to the evaluation of interventions aimed at disparities. In this vein, Rogers (2016, p. 199) summarizes, "Much of the discussion about addressing equity [in evaluation] focuses either on measuring unequal results or on using participatory approaches." I briefly review these approaches in this section but start with another historically common, but not totally satisfactory approach.

Many social and educational programs are targeted at people on the disadvantaged end of a disparity. In the United States, for example, the growth spurt of evaluation during the Great Society included evaluations of programs aimed at preschoolers from low-income families, schools with high proportions of youth with low academic performance, and adults who were unemployed. The evaluations examined whether program participants' outcomes improved relative to nonparticipants.

I use the term "targeted program" here for a program offered to those who are disadvantaged with respect to an outcome of interest (e.g., an educational intervention may be offered only to children with low educational performance). Alternatively, a targeted program may be offered to those who meet an eligibility criterion correlated with an outcome (e.g., a health program may be offered to people who fall below an income cutoff). When a targeted program is evaluated, generally a concern about a disparity is lurking about, even if this is not explicitly stated. Nevertheless, the findings of such an evaluation can be misleading as to whether the disparity was reduced. First, a targeted program may be beneficial compared to no program, but this may not be enough to overcome a tide of rising inequalities. Second, a program could be beneficial on average, but at the same time could increase disparities *among those eligible for the program.* That is, the program's benefits could have accrued primarily to the relatively better off of the eligible individuals, whereas the least well off are left behind. For these reasons, explicit attention to disparities is warranted.

One approach noted by Rogers focuses on conducting subgroup analyses, rather than only considering average treatment–comparison group differences. For instance, if a province implemented a new universal health care program, analyses would assess (among other things) whether there is less difference in health care outcomes after the program is implemented. Alternatively, the analyses might assess how much health care outcomes changed for different income subgroups (perhaps with comparisons to a neighboring province without the new program). The idea is to show that the difference across subgroups is reduced after the program. As another example, an evaluation of a new mathematics curriculum might compare effects across racial groups and across gender groups, examining whether disparities were reduced relative to the disparities in a comparison group.

Subgroup analyses can be conducted even when a targeted program is evaluated. One option is to stratify by initial standing on the outcome of interest. For example, if a program is designed to improve coronary health, analyses might compare people based on how poorly they scored initially on an index of heart health. Stratification could alternatively be done based on income, race, or other factors correlated with coronary health. The evaluator might also investigate subgroup difference in access to or uptake of the program services.

As Rogers points out, a second general approach advocated for equity-oriented evaluations is the use of participatory approaches. The argument for this is captured by the slogan, "Nothing about me, without me," from the disability rights and other movements. This fits well with one rationale for participatory approaches to evaluation in general, their potential for advancing social justice.

Of course, the two general approaches to disparities can be combined. A participatory evaluation can employ subgroup analyses that assess whether inequalities are lessened. Regardless of the evaluation approach taken, however, the evaluation is of questionable value if it does not contribute to social betterment in some way. Before turning to an approach for thinking about how to do this, I offer a comment on the evaluation capacity building (ECB) efforts described in earlier chapters.

Noble Endeavors

Chapters 1–5 of this volume derive from a major project intended to build evaluation capacity in China, especially around evaluations related to health inequity. At about the time, the capacity-building initiative was begun, a group of experts from the World Health Organization declared, "Evidence points to daunting [health] equity challenges for China" (Tang et al., 2008, p. 1493). China, of course, is the most populous country on Earth, with an estimated 18.8% of the world's population. Given the magnitude of the disparities involved, and given the large number of people affected, the importance of efforts such as those described in Chapters 1–5 seems rather obvious.

Chapters 6 and 7 are based on evaluations of health programs in India. India is the second most populous country on the planet (with an estimated 17.6% of the world's people) and also has substantial health disparities. Chapter 8 discusses lessons from a capacity-building effort in Chile. The chapters in this volume can be seen as a kind of comparative case study, with a rich tapestry of potential lessons for those interested in evaluation and social disparities.

One implicit lesson is that when ECB efforts are undertaken in many locations, practitioner and scholarly communities will have considerable expertise and relevant local knowledge, but may have limited (if any) experience with formal program evaluation. The hard won lessons of evaluation experience may not yet have been won there. This unsurprising observation makes ECB efforts both more important and more challenging. It is also another reason the model introduced in Chapter 1 rightly points to the need for a space for ongoing learning, including learning about ECB.

A Model of Evaluation Influence

Evaluations that attend to health inequities (or other discrepancies) will have little value if they make no difference in the way people think or act. Traditionally, concern about the consequences of evaluation has been discussed in terms of evaluation use. In recent years, evaluators have been encouraged to attend to "evaluation influence" (Henry & Mark, 2003; Kirkhart, 2000; Mark & Henry, 2004). Use often implies action that is intentional. Influence, in contrast, explicitly includes consequences of evaluation that are indirect and unintentional, perhaps removed from the evaluation in time or space, and perhaps without awareness of the influence on the part of the influenced person. For example, a parliamentarian who votes for a new program may have been indirectly influenced by an evaluation conducted in another jurisdiction. The evaluation findings may have led an aide to persuade the legislator to support the program, without the parliamentarian even knowing about the evaluation. Influence also explicitly includes unintended consequences of an evaluation. For example, an evaluation may have been commissioned with the idea of influencing local policy. But it may instead influence the redesign of the program or the design of a new program, perhaps at another location. This broader view of influence is consistent with Chapter 1 and other portions of the current volume.

Gary Henry and I (Henry & Mark, 2003; Mark, 2006; Mark & Henry, 2004) have discussed different possible categories of evaluation's consequences. The model is complicated, filling a 3 × 5 table with three "levels of analysis" combined with five "types of consequences." Several specific processes or consequences fall within each of the 15 cells of the 3 × 5 table. The editor of this volume asked me to consider the relevance of this model to health inequity related evaluations. In doing so, I present only a selective overview of the model of evaluation influence pathways.

The model distinguishes three levels of analysis: individual, interpersonal, and collective. Some consequences of evaluation are changes within a particular person (individual). Others involve interactions between individuals (interpersonal). Yet others occur at a more macro unit (collective). Think of these three in terms of the classic idea of direct or instrumental use. Imagine that an evaluation shows a pilot program reduced health inequities. One might hope that the evaluation would contribute to wider implementation of the program. In terms of the three levels of analysis, the desired change might involve: (a) individual physician's practices, such as when individual doctors adopt new health screening practices, or (b) the collective level, such as a governmental decision to expand funding for the intervention, or perhaps (c) the interpersonal level, such as a collaborative change in medical practices with health care professionals creating teams to promote increased access.

The preceding examples, such as passing a bill that funds a scaled-up program, represent changes that would in a sense be the desired end of evaluation influence. The phrase "in a sense" is important. Although most discussions about evaluation use and influence focus on possible changes such as a legislative vote or a change in practitioner behavior, these should not be considered ends in themselves. Rather, a change in practice or program scale is intended to lead to *improved outcomes for the intended beneficiaries*. With that in mind, I will call the change in practice or program the "near end-point" of evaluation influence.

A desired near end-point typically does not result directly from an evaluation. Instead, we can refer to influence pathways to capture the idea that interim steps, perhaps many interim steps, fall between the evaluation and the desired near end-point. Some of these interim steps may take place at different levels of analysis. To take a simplified example, an influence pathway might begin at the individual level, for instance, with an individual experiencing attitude change after hearing the evaluation results; this individual-level attitude changes might then stimulate interpersonal processes such as persuasion; and eventually those interpersonal persuasion processes might help bring about a collective decision, such as expanded program funding.

Levels of analysis are only part of the story of an influence pathway. In addition to the three levels of analysis, Mark & Henry (2004) identified four types of evaluation consequences. "Behavioral processes" are changes in actions. In the influence model, behavioral change is analogous to instrumental use but is broader, including actions indirectly influenced by the evaluation even if the person does not realize this (such as the example of the parliamentarian affected by her legislative aide). "Cognitive and affective processes" involve shifts in thoughts and feelings, such as attitude change. This influence category corresponds to classical concept of conceptual use or enlightenment, but again is broader (e.g., attitude change can take place without awareness of the evaluation as the initial source of influence). Behavioral processes and cognitive and affective processes can be the near end-point of an influence pathway, but they also can appear at various points in a multistep influence pathway.

Two of Mark and Henry's categories are probably of interest far more as possible steps along the pathway than as near end-point changes. "General influence processes" are relatively basic processes that may set into motion some other change along the pathway. For instance, at the individual level, elaboration is a process by which a person responds to a persuasive message or other input by thinking more deeply about an issue. Considerable research shows that elaboration can trigger long-lasting change in attitudes and thereby may lead to change in subsequent behaviors. Persuasion is a general influence process at the interpersonal level. Like general influence processes, "motivational processes" are expected to be interim steps rather than the desired end state of evaluation influence. Motivational processes involve goals, aspirations, and responses to perceived rewards and punishments, such as when reimbursement schedules are modified to increase individual physician's provision of childhood immunizations.

Mark (2006) added another category to the Mark and Henry (2004) framework. Tentatively labeled "relational consequences," this category includes changes, not in behavior, attitude, or motivation, but in aspects of relationships, structures, and organizational processes. The relational category would include the development of new alliances or collaborations or creation of a new forum for deliberation.

Putting the three levels of analysis together with the five types of mechanisms, 15 combinations, or cells in a table, result. Several specific mechanisms fall within each of the 15 cells. For example, for general influence processes at the interpersonal level, Mark and Henry (2004) listed justification, persuasion, change agent, and minority-opinion influence. The list of mechanisms, in a sense, is a catalog. It presents and categorizes a large array of processes and near end-point consequences of evaluation. Importantly, different subsets of these might be of interest across evaluations, when an evaluator creates a plan to try to optimize the likelihood of evaluation influence. Likewise, different processes or subsets of processes may be of interest in various research studies on evaluation influence.

Practice implications are lurking among the distinctions in this influence framework. As Henry and Mark (2003) suggest, the pathways that lead to individual or interpersonal change may be quite different than the pathways that lead to collective action (also see Weiss, 1998, pp. 264–265). For example, change in individual practitioner behavior may be more likely to involve motivational processes, such as when reimbursement schemes change the payoff for health care workers to attend to a particular problem. Also notable is that a given process may be the near end-point in one influence pathway but an interim step in another pathway. For example, collective action in the form of a legislative vote may be the near end endpoint for program expansion. But in another pathway a legislative vote may be an interim step that in turn changes reimbursement rates, with the hope that this will then motivate a change in practitioner behavior.

The Influence Model and Health Inequity Evaluation

In considering the application of the influence pathway model to health inequities, six general ideas come to mind: (a) certain mechanisms and pathways may be especially promising, as implied by the writing of other contributors to this volume; (b) evaluators can and, I would argue, should plan for influence pathways for their health disparity evaluations; (c) different practice settings may call for context-specific pathways; (d) the potential complexity of influence pathways deserves greater emphasis; (e) for practice, discussion of the possible mechanisms of influence needs accompanying attention to tangible procedures that should help set those processes in motion; and (f) the evaluation influence model has implications for ECB as well.

Promising Processes: Salience as an Example

Several of the contributors to this volume, in one fashion or another, alluded to evaluation's role in making health inequities more salient (see in particular Chapters 1, 2, and 6). For Mark and Henry (2004), salience is an individual-level phenomenon. Agenda setting is the collective analog. (Local descriptive norms are a comparable phenomenon at the interpersonal level, but probably less relevant process for health inequities.) Evaluations can help make inequities more salient and raise them on the policy agenda. For instance, policymakers and others may be more likely to think about health disparities if they are familiar with evaluations that include estimates of disparities. Increases in salience may be especially likely if evaluation reports and other communications about the evaluation skillfully highlight disparities, with compelling examples, meaningful statements about the magnitude of program effects in relation to the size of existing inequalities and thoughtful narratives.

This idea is consistent with Mark and Mills (2007) suggestion about expanding Patton's (1997) notion of process use to the broader "procedural influence." Process use refers to the possibility that direct participation in evaluation can have consequences, as in the idea that involvement in evaluation can lead to empowerment. The concept of procedural influence expands on this notion by including effects of evaluation procedures on those who did not directly participate in the evaluation. When disparities are explicitly measured, when evaluation findings are reported in terms of inequity reduction, and when compelling examples are used, health inequities can be made more salient among those who hear about the evaluation. If evaluations make health inequities more salient generally, this could well contribute to long-term consequences, even if these effects may be distant in time and detail.

The numerous individual processes of the 15-celled table from Mark and Henry (2004) and Mark (2006) could each be reviewed in terms of their possible role in attempts to make an evaluation influential. Consider elaboration as another example. Elaboration occurs when an individual thinks about a message and reflects on it. Elaboration is more likely to occur when the individual is both motivated and able to process the message. An evaluator seeking to increase evaluation influence might think about how to increase the motivation and ability of relevant parties to engage in sense-making about the key messages from their evaluation (such as whether the program reduced health inequalities). With further experience, training on such matters might be incorporated into future ECB efforts.

Planning Influence Pathways

The road from evaluation to a desired near end-point will usually involve multiple intermediate processes. The influence model invites evaluators to try to draw out the pathway (or pathways) by which an evaluation can be influential. Consider a simplified example. A briefing about evaluation findings might have the following effects: (a) a legislative aide in attendance might engage in elaboration, thinking about the evaluation finding, reflecting on the briefing and adding her own thoughts; (b) the elaboration process in turn may lead the legislative aide to have a more positive attitude toward the program; (c) given this positive attitude, the aide may engage in interpersonal processes such as persuasion efforts directed at other legislative staff and at her boss; (d) these interpersonal persuasion processes might eventually contribute to the inclusion of language that expands program funding in an omnibus spending bill; and (e) passage of the bill may lead to collective-level policy change. For influence pathways, the metaphor is of a set of dominoes, sitting upright, with the first domino needing to fall to knock down the second domino, the second to knock down the third, and so on, to reach the near end-point such as policy change. Or, if the sequence is interrupted (or based on implausible assumptions) and, say, the third domino does not knock over the fourth, the pathway will fail to reach the desired near end-point.

Thinking about pathways, rather than individual processes, should be beneficial. Evaluators can think about the chain of events that need to occur, and within limits of feasibility and evaluator role, evaluators can think about what they—and possibly others—can do to help the various processes take place. Again, with further experience, future ECB might attend to such matters.

The Potential Need for Context-Specific Influence Processes and Pathways

The specific circumstances surrounding an evaluation may well affect the kind of pathway through which evaluation influence may occur. For example, one evaluation may be conducted at the request of a person or agency with the capacity to act on the results. In another instance, the evaluation may be commissioned by someone who would not play a role in acting on the results; in addition, authority to act may be diffused across multiple parties with varied interests and perspectives. The pathway to the desired near end-state is likely to be longer and less certain in the latter case.

This volume includes contributions involving evaluation and ECB in China, India, and Chile. These countries have important differences, including differences in political structure and national history. Even within a single country, the governing regime and national priorities may be considerably different when an evaluation is over, compared to when it was conceived. Such differences likely will have implications, potentially major implications, for influence pathways. Certain fundamental processes, like elaboration and persuasion, are likely to apply across settings, though the parties who need to be involved may differ substantially. On the other hand, collective processes may differ in fundamental ways across countries with different governing systems and structures. Studies of influence pathways in various contexts, especially cross-national studies, would be informative. Fortunately when it comes to practice, savvy nationals will have a good sense of the relevant collective processes.

Recognizing the Complicated Nature of the Influence Environment

The metaphor of dominos, used earlier, could seem to suggest a single, linear process. The reality is likely to be more complex, however. Mark and Henry (2004, p. 48) noted that "the pathways to evaluation influence will often be complex and even circuitous, involving the concatenation of multiple mechanisms." They also noted that evaluation influence "takes place within a market-place of competing information and values. Other forces, such as program clients, advocacy organizations and partisan politicians often engage in influence processes that pull in a different direction than evaluation .... [Also,] All change processes are contingent, in that they will operate in some circumstances and not others."

These complications are especially likely to apply in areas such as health inequities, especially in a political system without strong general support on the priority of reducing health disparities. As noted by contributors to this volume, especially in Chapter 2, the near end-point suggested by evaluation may conflict with other values held by policymakers. Other policy issues may take priority and distract attention from health equities. Regimes may change or support for reducing disparities may wane for other reasons.

For these and related reasons, planning a single evaluation pathway will often be inadequate. Planning more than one pathway may be better. In addition, planned pathways may well need to be supplemented with more emergent influence efforts, either when the initial plan goes awry or when an unexpected opportunity arises (e.g., a major news story appears that involves health inequities and could stimulate attention to the results of a recent evaluation). Moreover, for topics as multifaceted as health inequities, any single evaluation will often be inadequate to tilt important actions. Instead, evaluators may need to seek to increase the (appropriate) influence of their evaluation, while integrating findings from other evaluations and from other evidence. They may need to think of the proper influence of evaluation, not as the responsibility of the evaluator, but as a shared responsibility of a community of evaluators and others. This seems consistent with aspects of the overarching framework of this volume, such as the idea of a "space of deliberation" in Figure 1 of the Editors' Notes and elsewhere.

Practices as well as Processes

The Mark and Henry influence model lists processes, such as elaboration, persuasion, and agenda setting, that have been addressed by scholars in various areas of inquiry. For evaluation practice, it is important to be able to translate these possible influence processes into tangible procedures. This can involve, for example, specific steps to try to ensure that people who learn about an evaluation's findings are given motivation to think about the findings and that the findings are presented in a way that enables evaluation consumers to elaborate on them.

In some instances, practice-oriented procedures will involve creating circumstances that might facilitate the initiation of multiple processes. For example, in a study based on the Mark and Henry influence framework, Gildemyn (2014) found that having a formal forum for the discussion of evaluation findings was associated with more influence processes occurring. A deliberative space of the kind Gildemyn investigated can provide increased opportunities for elaboration, persuasion (and planning for persuasion), statements of commitment that should help motivate subsequent action, and other influence processes. Again, this idea is consistent with the idea of a "space of deliberation" in Figure 1 of the Editors' Notes and elsewhere in this volume.

The Evaluation Influence Model and ECB

Especially with further experience, the influence model could be among the topics considered in ECB efforts. I have already noted the possibility of attending to individual processes, such as salience and elaboration, and to multiprocess evaluation pathways when doing ECB. The influence model can also be used when thinking about working with funders to obtain support for ECB itself.

At its simplest, the core idea of evaluation pathways is to think about evaluation as an intervention in the world, and to incorporate thinking analogous to a program theory or theory of change to plan and account for the possible consequences of evaluation. In similar fashion, one could think about building influence pathways to help garner support for ECB. For example, a chain might involve making the need for ECB salient, engaging in persuasion efforts with relevant parties, and supporting whatever collective-level processes are needed to fund future ECB efforts.

Conclusion

The chapters in this volume deserve to be influential. I encourage readers to elaborate on their lessons, engage in dialog with colleagues, and consider implication for collective action regarding equity oriented evaluations and ECB.

The overarching framework of this volume, laid out in the Editors' Notes and Chapter 1, suggests the need for an ongoing process and space for learning. This applies, not only to learning about inequities and about the evaluation of inequities, but also to the theories and practices we draw on to try to achieve the appropriate influence of evaluation that focus on disparities. I hope a growing body of evaluators will join that space.

References

Bamberger, M., & Segone, M. (2014). *How to design and manage equity-focused evaluations*. Washington, DC: UNICEF.

Donaldson, S. I., & Picciotto, R. (2016). *Evaluation for an equitable society*. Charlotte, NC: Information Age Publishing.

Gildemyn, M. (2014). Understanding the influence of independent civil society monitoring and evaluation at the district level: A case study of Ghana. *American Journal of Evaluation, 35*, 507–524.

Henry, G. T., & Mark, M. M. (2003). Beyond use: Understanding evaluation's influence on attitudes and actions. *American Journal of Evaluation, 24*, 294–314.

Kirkhart, K. E. (2000). Reconceptualizing evaluation use: An integrated theory of influence. *New Directions for Evaluation*, 5–23. https://doi.org/10.1002/ev.1188

Mark, M. M. (2006). *The consequences of evaluation: Theory, research, and practice.* Presidential address Evaluation 2006: Annual meeting of the American Evaluation Association, Portland, OR.

Mark, M. M., & Henry, G. T. (2004). The mechanisms and outcomes of evaluation influence. *Evaluation, 10*(1), 35–57.

Mark, M. M., & Mills, J. (2007). The use of experiments and quasi-experiments in decision making. In G. Morcöl (Ed.), *Handbook of decision making* (pp. 459–482). New York: Marcel Dekker.

Patton, M. Q. (1997) *Utilization-focused Evaluation: The New Century Text.* Thousand Oaks, CA: Sage.

Piketty, T. (2013). *Capital in the twenty-first century.* Cambridge, MA: Harvard University Press.

Piketty, T. (2015). *The economics of inequality.* Cambridge, MA: Harvard University Press.

Rogers, P. J. (2016). Understanding and supporting equity: Implications of methodological and procedural choices in equity-focused evaluations. In S. I. Donaldson & R. Picciotto (Eds.), *Evaluation for an equitable society.* Charlotte, NC: Information Age Publishing.

Tang, S., Meng, Q., Chen, L., Bekedam, H., Evans, T., & Whitehead, M. (2008). Health system reform in China 1: Tackling the challenges to health equity in China. *Lancet,* Oct 25, *372*(9648), 1493-1501. Published online, October 20, 2008. https://doi.org/10.1016/S0140-6736(08)61364-1

UNICEF. (2012). *Evaluation for equitable development results.* New York: UNICEF.

United Nations. (2015). *Transforming our world: The 2030 Agenda for Sustainable Development.* New York: United Nations.

Weiss, C. H. (1998). Improving the use of evaluations: Whose job is it anyway? *Advances in Educational Productivity, 7,* 263-276.

MELVIN M. MARK *is professor and head of psychology at Penn State University, a former president of the American Evaluation Association, former editor of the* American Journal of Evaluation, *and past recipient of AEA's Lazarsfeld Award for Evaluation Theory.*

INDEX

NEW DIRECTIONS FOR EVALUATION

ORDER FORM SUBSCRIPTION AND SINGLE ISSUES

DISCOUNTED BACK ISSUES:

Use this form to receive 20% off all back issues of *New Directions for Evaluation*.
All single issues priced at **$23.20** (normally $29.00)

TITLE	ISSUE NO.	ISBN

Call 1-800-835-6770 or see mailing instructions below. When calling, mention the promotional code JBNND to receive your discount. For a complete list of issues, please visit www.wiley.com/WileyCDA/WileyTitle/productCd-EV.html

SUBSCRIPTIONS: (1 YEAR, 4 ISSUES)

☐ New Order   ☐ Renewal

U.S.	☐ Individual: $89	☐ Institutional: $380
CANADA/MEXICO	☐ Individual: $89	☐ Institutional: $422
ALL OTHERS	☐ Individual: $113	☐ Institutional: $458

Call 1-800-835-6770 or see mailing and pricing instructions below.
Online subscriptions are available at www.onlinelibrary.wiley.com

ORDER TOTALS:

Issue / Subscription Amount: $ _____

Shipping Amount: $ _____
(for single issues only – subscription prices include shipping)

Total Amount: $ _____

SHIPPING CHARGES:
First Item $6.00
Each Add'l Item $2.00

(No sales tax for U.S. subscriptions. Canadian residents, add GST for subscription orders. Individual rate subscriptions must be paid by personal check or credit card. Individual rate subscriptions may not be resold as library copies.)

BILLING & SHIPPING INFORMATION:

☐ **PAYMENT ENCLOSED:** *(U.S. check or money order only. All payments must be in U.S. dollars.)*

☐ **CREDIT CARD:**   ☐ VISA   ☐ MC   ☐ AMEX

Card number _____Exp. Date_____

Card Holder Name_____Card Issue # _____

Signature _____Day Phone_____

☐ **BILL ME:** *(U.S. institutional orders only. Purchase order required.)*

Purchase order # _____
Federal Tax ID 13559302 • GST 89102-8052

Name_____

Address_____

Phone_____ E-mail_____

Copy or detach page and send to: **John Wiley & Sons, Inc. / Jossey Bass**
PO Box 55381
Boston, MA 02205-9850

PROMO JBNND